# THE DOCTOR WORE PETTICOATS

## WOMEN PHYSICIANS OF THE OLD WEST

"The profiles of these women are poignant, enlightening and inspiring—from Doc Susie Anderson of Colorado, my personal favorite, who found herself fighting an uphill battle in the mining camp of Cripple Creek, to Flora Haywood Stanford, who was the first female doctor in Deadwood and treated residents such as Calamity Jane and Buffalo Bill."

—Linda Wommack, *True West*

# THE DOCTOR WORE PETTICOATS

## WOMEN PHYSICIANS OF THE OLD WEST

Chris Enss

## TWODOT®

GUILFORD, CONNECTICUT
HELENA, MONTANA
AN IMPRINT OF THE GLOBE PEQUOT PRESS

A · T W O D O T® · B O O K

Copyright © 2006 by Chris Enss

Text design: Lisa Reneson

**Library of Congress Cataloging-in-Publication Data**
Enss, Chris, 1961-
  The doctor wore petticoats : women physicians of the old West / Chris Enss.–1st ed.
      p. cm.
  Includes bibliographical references.
  ISBN 978-0-7627-3566-2
1. Women physicians–West (U.S.)–Biography. 2. Medicine–West (U.S.)–History. I. Title.
R692.E67 2006
610'.92'278–dc22                                  2005023247


Printed in the United States of America
First Edition/Sixth Printing

*For my mother-in-law Norma, for never failing to inspire and encourage everyone she comes in contact with*

# CONTENTS

# ACKNOWLEDGMENTS

The historical records of the women doctors of the Old West exist because of archivists dedicated to preserving the accounts of these courageous female pioneers. They are owed a debt of gratitude and deserve to be recognized for their efforts in helping to make this book possible. With that in mind I offer sincere thanks to the following organizations:

Nevada State Library & Archives Department
California State Library History Room
Oregon Historical Society
Nebraska State Historical Society
Utah History Research Center
National Library of Medicine
Penfield Gallery of Indian Arts
New Mexico Library & Archives Department
University of Mexico Education Department
San Francisco, California Historical Society
Kansas State Archives Department
National Archives Department, Washington, D.C.
Adams House Historical Staff, Deadwood, South Dakota
Denver Public Library
Library of Congress
Nevada County Library

I'd like to offer a special thanks to Debra Chapman-Luckinbill for supplying the photographs of her great-great-grandmother, Nellie Pooler Chapman, and to Priscilla Newcomb for the use of the photograph of her mother, Franc Johnson Newcomb.

I'd also like to thank the editors and staff at The Globe Pequot Press for their ability to take the raw material submitted to them and transform it into a quality product. I am consistently impressed with the process and the outcome.

# INTRODUCTION

---

*Higher education for women produces monstrous brains and puny bodies; abnormally active cerebration and abnormally weak digestion; flowing thought and constipated bowel.*
— E. H. Clarke, *Sex Education:*
*A Fair Chance for Girls,* 1873

The frontier of the wild West resisted attempts to tame it by adventurous pioneers who were hell-bent on making a life for themselves and their families on the open range. The terrain was rough and unyielding, not unlike its new inhabitants. Most of these inhabitants were as stubborn about accepting female doctors as the land was about accepting them.

Women in the mid-1800s who possessed a strong desire to help the sick studied, worked, and struggled for places in medical schools. After receiving their degrees they studied, worked, and struggled to find a place to practice their vocation. The western frontier, with its absence of physicians and high demand for healthcare, provided women the opportunity to open medical offices. It did not, however, assure them patients. For a while it seemed most trappers, miners, and emigrants would rather suffer and die than consult a woman doctor. The lady doctor repairing a head wound on an injured farmer in the nineteenth and early twentieth centuries would have had to endure criticism from skeptics and male physicians who believed women shouldn't be in the profession at all.

# INTRODUCTION

Male doctors hoping to prevent the "fairer sex" from entering the field of medicine publicly chastised those women who had such desires. They often referred to them as "unnatural" and "lacking in the ability to know their place." A protest resolution drafted by male students at Harvard University in 1850 summed up the position of many men on the subject:

> *Resolved, That no woman of true delicacy would be willing in the presence of men to listen to the discussions of the subjects that necessarily come under the consideration of the student of medicine.*
>
> *Resolved, That we object to having the company of any female forced upon us, who is disposed to unsex herself, and to sacrifice her modesty by appearing with men in the medical lecture room.*

An article that appeared in an 1867 New York medical journal boldly announced that male physicians

> *hope to never see a day when the female character shall be so completely unsexed, as to fit it for the disgusting duties which imperatively devolve upon one who would attain proficiency, or even respectability in the healing art.*

In the mid- to late nineteenth century, as the country continued expanding its boundaries beyond Independence, Missouri, in a quest to civilize the wild frontier, there were fewer than 600 women physicians in the United States. Ten percent of those female doctors decided to follow the migration and offer their services to the emigrants in the West.

These women, who dared defy the sexual barriers in the

medical profession to attend school and acquire a degree, were convinced settlers would eventually seek their counsel and they brazenly opened offices in frontier towns and mining camps. The result of these few courageous women braving hardship and prejudice was a change in the way society viewed women's roles and the improvement of the health of many settlers.

Doctor Eliza Cook had a strong impact on the male-dominated community in Carson Valley, Nevada. Men who felt women were "not blessed with the temperament or disposition to be doctors" changed their minds after years of watching Doctor Cook work. The tall, slender lady from Salt Lake City, Utah, set broken limbs, performed operations, and delivered generations of babies in the small northern Nevada town where she lived. She was not only a skilled physician but also a pharmacist, and she contributed numerous articles to medical journals and magazines on a variety of health related issues. She is considered by many historians to have been the first woman doctor in Nevada.

Another daring female physician to practice in the American West was Doctor Minnie Frances Hayden Howard. After attending Kansas City Medical College, Doctor Howard established a practice in Pocatello, Idaho. She not only cared for the ailing in the booming gold-mining camp but also tended to the health needs of the Native Americans in the area, and eventually helped build the Pocatello General Hospital.

In time the wild frontier would become civilized. Many tough-minded women doctors like Eliza Cook and Frances Howard, would pour onto the western plains, paving the way for other professional women yet to come.

In Cripple Creek, Colorado, Doctor Susan Anderson set up her practice and helped save the lives of many sick and injured gold miners. Doctor Flora Hayward Stanford braved the wild and wooly town of Deadwood, South Dakota, to tend to such patients as Calamity Jane and Buffalo Bill Cody. Doctor Georgia Arbuckle Fix defied the wishes of her puritanical husband to serve the medical needs of settlers in western Nebraska. Women like Nellie Pooler Chapman and Lucy Hobbs Taylor struggled along the path of prejudice to become the West's leading ladies in the field of dentistry.

Female physicians were subjected to more than scorn and ridicule when they decided to practice their vocation; they oftentimes risked life and limb. Women medical students and graduated doctors were discouraged by law enforcement from calling on patients at night in big cities like San Francisco, for fear they would be attacked by resentful male colleagues. Sometimes, female physicians like Lillian Heath of Wyoming, who did risk going out, wore men's clothing to hide their gender.

The medical experts highlighted in this volume paid a personal price to bring about changes in healthcare, but their efforts would solidify their place in medicine and encourage others to follow in their footsteps. One hundred years after the first American female physician, Elizabeth Blackwell, graduated from medical school in 1849, only a little over 5 percent of students entering the field were women. But female physicians of the nineteenth century, like Bethenia Owens-Adair and Georgia Arbuckle Fix, dug the trail for future generations of female doctors to come. Twentieth-century women physicians such as Gerty Cori, the Nobel Prize winner for Physiology and Medicine, and Mae Jemison, astronaut and medical officer for NASA's space program, made tremendous advances in the medical profession and paved the way for other females.

Women who have followed these pioneering doctors into medicine owe much to the great strides made by their predecessors. As surgeon Marie Mergler said of the fight for equal access to training for women and for respect in their chosen profession, "it meant much more than success or failure for the individual; it meant the failure or success of a grand cause." *The Doctor Wore Petticoats* examines the lives of but a few women endowed with the stamina needed to one day earn the title of Doctor.

# BETHENIA OWENS-ADAIR

## NORTHWEST PHYSICIAN

*I am determined to get at least a common education. I now know
that I can support and educate myself and my boy, and I am
resolved to do it; furthermore, I do not intend to do it over a
washtub either.*

—Bethenia Owens-Adair, 1874

A loud rap on the door of the hat shop coaxed the diminutive
young woman from her work of loading bolts of fabric into a trunk.
The scruffy messenger on the other side of the door smiled politely
when Bethenia Owens greeted him, and then handed her a letter.
The monogram on the envelope showed that the correspondence
came from Doctor Palmer, a prominent physician in the
northwestern area of the United States.

The messenger waited patiently for Bethenia to break the seal
on the envelope and read the enclosed note. "How sad," she said to
no one in particular. "One of our elder citizens passed away . . . and
the six local physicians who treated him at one time or another
want to do an autopsy. And as one of the newest doctors in town,
I'm invited to attend the operation." The messenger grinned and
nodded, anticipating a negative response.

Bethenia knew the invitation was meant as a joke and was determined to turn the tables on the pranksters. There were very few

women in medicine in 1872, and, by and large, they were not well received by men in the same profession.

Bethenia studied the note, carefully considering the proper response. "Give Doctor Palmer and the others my regards," she announced. "And tell them I'll be there in a few minutes." A stunned look fell over the courier's face as he turned and hurried off down the dusty thoroughfare in Roseburg, Oregon.

Bethenia followed, a safe distance behind the messenger, to Doctor Palmer's office, where she waited outside. She listened in as the courier relayed the information she had given him and heard the doctors laughing heartily. Bethenia opened the door, momentarily interrupting their merriment. One of the doctors regained his composure and walked toward her with his hand outstretched. She shook it and the physician choked back a giggle.

"Do you know the autopsy is on the genital organs?" he snickered. "No," Bethenia replied, "But one part of the human body should be as sacred to the physician as another." The mood in the room quickly changed to one of disbelief and then, in an instant, to indignation.

Doctor Palmer objected to Bethenia's presence during the procedure and insisted that he would leave if she stayed. Bethenia was unmoved by the pronouncement and stood her ground. "I came here by written invitation," she calmly confessed. "I will leave it to a vote whether I go or stay; but first I would like to ask Doctor Palmer what is the difference between the attendance of a woman at a male autopsy and the attendance of a man at a female autopsy?"

For a few moments none of the male physicians replied. She had presented to them a sensible query, demonstrating her dedication to the profession and a maturity they had underestimated. One by one, the men slowly voted in favor of Bethenia not only staying, but of performing the procedure as well.

News of Bethenia's brave stand circulated throughout the lumber town. A number of curious onlookers, including the messenger, lined the street to get a look at the strange female doctor as she exited the office. Many citizens strongly disapproved of a woman in that line of work, and had it not been for her family members, the scene would have likely erupted into violence.

Not long after the much-talked-about event, Bethenia completed the task of closing her milliner business, moved to northern Oregon with her sister, and started her own medical practice. Physicians, male or female, were woefully lacking in many parts of the West. Doctor Owens hoped the need for her skills in Portland would far outweigh any reservations people might have had regarding her gender.

From a very early age, Bethenia exercised her individuality and proved herself a pioneer in many circumstances. She was born in Missouri, on February 7, 1840. Her father and eight siblings emigrated to Oregon in 1843 and settled in Clatsop County. By the time she turned eighteen, she had been married, divorced, and had a son. She supported herself and her child by taking in laundry—work suitable for women, but objectionable to Bethenia's father, who offered to take care of his daughter and his grandson. Bethenia steadfastly refused such monetary help from her family, but did accept the sewing machine her parents gave her. After teaching herself to be a seamstress, she added mending to her list of services for hire.

Bethenia's formal education was limited. At the age of sixteen, she could barely read and write. Anxious to learn and better herself, she leapt at an offer from a good friend in nearby Oysterville, Washington, to attend school there. Bethenia worked her way through primary school by doing laundry for ranch hands. Through books and lessons she overcame the hardships associated with a failed marriage and single parenthood. In 1874, she wrote:

> *Thus passed one of the pleasantest, and most profitable winters of my life, while, whetted by what it fed on, my desire for knowledge grew daily stronger.*

An urgent plea from Bethenia's sister persuaded her to leave Washington and return to Clatsop County. Bethenia agreed to help her ailing sister in exchange for the chance to attend and teach school in Astoria. After arriving back in Oregon, Bethenia immediately went to work soliciting students for a summer-school term. Her dauntless will and determination are evident in Bethenia's recollection of the experience:

> *I succeeded in getting the promise of sixteen pupils, for which I was to receive $2 for three months. This was my first attempt to instruct others. I taught my school in the Old Presbyterian Church, the first Presbyterian Church building ever erected in Oregon.*
>
> *Of my sixteen pupils there were three who were more advanced than myself, but I took their books home with me nights and with the help of my brother-in-law I managed to prepare the lessons beforehand, and they never suspected my incompetency.*

In the fall of 1861, Bethenia again enrolled in school. The principal of the institution assisted her with her work when needed. She awoke at four o'clock every morning to study, determined to take full advantage of the "great opportunity" she had been given.

Within nine months Bethenia had completed her high school education. Before and after attending classes, she kept up with her variety of labor-intensive jobs and gave special attention to her son.

Bethenia's thirst for knowledge did not subside after graduation. Her fondness for nursing and caring for sick friends and family sparked a desire to study medicine. Her superior talent in hat design and dressmaking helped her to raise the necessary funds to attend medical school. She became truly committed to the calling after witnessing an elderly doctor's inability to care properly for a small child:

> *The old physician in my presence attempted to use an instrument for the relief of the little sufferer, and, in his long, bungling, and unsuccessful attempt he severely lacerated the tender flesh of the poor little girl. At last, he laid down the instrument, to wipe his glasses. I picked it up saying, "Let me try, Doctor," and passed it instantly, with perfect ease, bringing immediate relief to the tortured child.*

That momentous event set in motion the course of Bethenia's new profession.

Words of encouragement for Bethenia's goal were few and far between, however. In fact, once she made her career plans known, only two people supported her. One was a trusted physician, who loaned her his medical books; the other was a judge, who applauded her ambition and assured her that she "would win." Most of Bethenia's family and friends were opposed to her becoming a doctor. They sneered and laughed and told her it was a disgrace for a woman to enter into such work. Bethenia disregarded their warnings and criticism, and pressed on toward her objective.

Bethenia began her studies at the Philadelphia Eclectic School of Medicine in 1870. Students at the college learned ways to treat the sick using herbs, mineral baths, and natural medicines. After a two-year absence from her home and son George, who was with her parents, Bethenia returned to Roseburg eager to set up a practice. The controversy that surrounded her after the autopsy incident, however, forced her to open an office in Portland instead. The ground floor of her Portland facilities had two rooms that she fitted for eclectic and medicated baths. Several patients sought out her unorthodox method of dealing with sickness and pain, and in no time, her business was making a profit. Bethenia could then afford to send nineteen-year-old George to the UC Berkeley Medical School. He graduated in 1874.

Although Doctor Owens's eclectic medical practice was prosperous, she was not satisfied. She pined for more knowledge in her chosen field. On September 1, 1878, she left Portland for Philadelphia, to seek counsel from a professor at her former college. She was advised to attend the University of Michigan, and she left at once to enroll:

> Arriving there, I was soon settled, and in my seat for the opening lecture. . . . During the ensuing nine months, I averaged sixteen hours a day in attending lectures, in hard study, and in all exercises required in the courses, after which I put in ten hours a day (except Sundays) in study during vacation.

Her daily schedule was filled with lectures, clinics, laboratory work, and examinations. Bethenia was so engrossed in her studies that she did not hear the bell ring between classes. She never tired of the learning process and she never suffered with a day of sickness.

In June of 1880, Doctor Owens received her second degree. After graduation she traveled with one of her classmates to do field work in hospitals and clinics in Chicago. In the fall of that same year, she returned to the University of Michigan, accompanied by her son. Together, the mother and son doctors attended advanced lectures in obstetrics and homeopathic remedies. Six months after their arrival, they embarked on a trip abroad. Their European tour included visits to Hamburg, Munich, Paris, and England. It was a welcome change of pace for Bethenia, who by then had been continually working and studying for more than thirty years.

Doctor Owens settled in San Francisco after her journey across the sea, and it was there she met her second husband. Before she met Colonel John Adair, Bethenia maintained that she was fully committed to her profession and not interested in marriage. A brief courtship with the handsome Civil War veteran changed her mind. The two were married on July 24, 1884, in Portland, Oregon. Three years after the wedding, the Adairs were expecting their first child. Bethenia boasted in her journal that she was happier than she had ever been before. Her elation would not last long:

> *At the age of forty-seven I gave birth to a little daughter; and now my joy knew no limit, my cup of bliss was full to overflowing. A son I had, and a daughter was what I most desired. . . . For three days only, was she left with us, and then my treasure was taken from me, to join in the immortal hosts beyond all earthly pain and sorrow.*

Bethenia found solace from the grief of her daughter's death in caring for the sick in her Portland practice. No matter what the weather conditions were, and knowing that there was no other

# HUMAN STERILIZATION

DR. B. OWENS ADAIR, Author of The Famous

"HUMAN STERILIZATION" BILL

of Oregon

THREE YEARS AFTER BETHENIA OWENS-ADAIR PUBLISHED "HUMAN STERILIZATION: ITS SOCIAL AND LEGISLATIVE ASPECTS," OREGON PASSED ITS STERILIZATION BILL.

doctor within a 200-mile radius, she never refused a call from a patient. She attended to all those in need, at times traveling through dense undergrowth and swollen rivers.

Never content with being solely a physician, Bethenia became a student again in 1889 and enrolled in a Chicago medical school, seeking a post-graduate degree. After she completed her studies, she returned home to her husband and the teenage son they had adopted. Her practice continued to grow, and before long she found she could not keep up with her professional work and maintain a home for her family. She chose the practice over her marriage and sent John away to a farm they owned in Astoria. The Adairs' marriage ended in 1903.

At the age of sixty-five, Bethenia retired from her practice. Her focus then shifted from day-to-day medical treatment to research. She studied such controversial topics as the sterilization of the criminally insane. Bethenia's analysis led her to believe that insanity and criminal action were hereditary. Her famous work on the subject, entitled "Human Sterilization: Its Social and Legislative Aspects," was published in 1922, and brought her instant recognition in the field. Three years after Adair presented her findings, a sterilization statute was adopted as state law in Oregon.

In addition to her medical research, Bethenia worked hard as a lobbyist for the Women's Christian Temperance Union. She remained a staunch social and political activist until 1926, when she died of natural causes at the age of eighty-six.

# GEORGIA ARBUCKLE FIX

## FRONTIER SURGEON

*Under the care of Doctor Arbuckle Fix any person can be expected to be nearly raised from the dead.*

—*Gering Courier,* May 1889

A lone rider urged her horse up a steep embankment and into a stand of large cottonwoods. Although it was daytime, the tree covering gave an effect of an almost cathedral-like darkness. Doctor Georgia Arbuckle Fix shifted in her saddle, then checked to make sure her medical bag was still tied to the horn. She sighed a tired sigh as she cast a glance into the valley and at her home near the town of Gering, Nebraska, in the distance.

In 1886, Georgia Arbuckle was the only doctor in a 75-mile radius of Gering. She was accustomed to traveling long miles across the open frontier to see patients. On this particular day she had been summoned to the home of a farmer and his pregnant wife. Georgia smiled to herself as she remembered the look on the young parents' faces as they welcomed their child into the world. She looked at her pocket watch, then spurred her horse into a bit of a trot.

The glare from the sun blinded Georgia's view of the road as she exited the trees. She did not see the bearded highwayman lying in wait for her. The toothless crook threw up his hands.

*Nebraska State Historical Society*

By the time she was fifteen years old, Georgia Arbuckle had completed high school and obtained a teaching certificate. Soon after, she enrolled in medical school.

Georgia's horse reared a bit and she eased the animal into a full stop.

The man stumbled. Laughing, he reached for a nearby outcropping of rocks to steady himself. The empty bottles of whisky around his makeshift camp led Georgia to assess that the robber was drunk. He made his way over to her and attempted to pull her off the horse. She tried to kick him away, but he had a stubborn hold on her leg. The fearless, thirty-four–year-old woman quickly released the buckle on the harness that was holding her medical bag, grabbed the case by the handle, and knocked the thief across the head with it. The man yelped and staggered about like a decapitated chicken. Georgia coaxed her horse into a gallop and hurried off.

Doctor Arbuckle Fix's willingness to risk her own life to save the life of others left a lasting impression on the people in Douglas County, Nebraska.

Georgia Arbuckle was born in Princeton, Missouri, on April 26. Missouri census records list the year of her birth as 1850, but school enrollment forms show that she was born in 1852. Historians speculate that the confusion surrounding her year of birth began with Georgia herself. After learning the enrollment age for medical school was thirty, she changed the year to fit the criteria.

Georgia's mother was Julia Ann Arbuckle. The identity of her father was never revealed to her. Thomas Reeves married Julia Ann in 1859 and raised Georgia as his own. He recognized a "keen sense of intelligence and drive" in his adopted daughter, and encouraged her to "always seek after knowledge." By the time Georgia was fifteen, she had graduated from high school and acquired a teaching certificate, and was teaching school at a log building near the family home.

Georgia's talent for learning and sharing knowledge captured the attention of the local physician, Doctor Dinsmore, who persuaded the teenager to study homeopathic medicine. The doctor's eager student excelled in the field, and her interest in medicine grew.

Doctor Dinsmore invited his protégé to move to Nebraska with him and his wife. There, Georgia could assist her mentor in his practice and attend medical school. She eagerly agreed and in 1881 enrolled at the University of Omaha.

Georgia was one of eight students to register to become a doctor. She was the only woman. After graduating in 1883, she opened her own practice. The following year she agreed to serve on the board of the Douglas County Medical Society.

In May 1886, Georgia followed her brother and stepfather to western Nebraska. Taken in by the beauty of the land and its wide-open spaces, she settled down on a forty-acre homestead along the North Platte River, near Gering. After building herself a home, she offered her services to the sick and ailing in the community. She was called to attend to ranchers with broken bones and torn flesh, children with the flu and pneumonia, and the elderly suffering with arthritis.

The novelty of a woman doctor on the male-dominated frontier did not escape the attention of the curious westerners. Georgia once responded to a call to set a cowboy's broken limb. After riding 18 miles, she found that the man wasn't hurt at all; he merely wanted to see a lady doctor. Doctor Arbuckle charged the man for the visit and scolded him for keeping her from someone who might really be in need.

In 1888, a legitimate call to help a deathly ill man with typhoid fever changed the young doctor's life. When she arrived at the patient's home, the man introduced himself as Gwynn Fix. The two were quite smitten with one another. Georgia was attracted to Gwynn's soft voice, blue eyes, and black hair. He was charmed by her kindness and her attention. Within six months after they met, the two were married. After a short honeymoon at Georgia's place, the Fixes moved their home to a tree-lined plot of land 7 miles away. Gwynn worked the land and Georgia continued on with her practice. For a while they were happy.

Oftentimes, the patients in Doctor Arbuckle Fix's practice did not pay her in dollars and cents. She was paid in wood for her stove, fresh fruit, poultry, eggs, butter, and cattle. Five years after Georgia opened her medical practice, she had earned thousands of eggs, a flock of chickens, and more than one hundred head of cattle. Gwynn was pleased with his wife's success, but he was becoming increasingly frustrated with the time she spent away from him while she was doing her job.

He felt that Georgia should cut back on her workload and devote herself to creating a proper home, but Georgia lacked the talent and the desire to live out her days as a traditional housewife. She was beyond child-bearing years and acutely aware of the many medical needs in Douglas County. She was unwilling to give Gwynn what he wanted, and the marriage suffered greatly as a result. Gwynn's attention shifted from Georgia to politics and visits to the saloon. As he drifted further and further away, Georgia focused more and more on her patients.

The lack of medical supplies in the rural area forced Doctor Arbuckle Fix to create inventive ways to handle serious injuries. She set a busted hand using a shingle for a splint, and mended a fractured skull using a coin as a protective plate. On those rare occasions when Georgia lost a patient, she attended to their needs after they had passed away. Compassionate to the end, she helped with the burial and even gave the eulogy.

Her reputation as a doctor was solid, but as a wife it was shaky. The more time she spent away from Gwynn on house calls, the more gossip circulated that she was involved with another man. Gwynn generated much of the gossip himself. By 1909, Doctor Arbuckle Fix had had enough and filed for divorce. Gwynn countersued and before the scandal could be resolved, he left the county, taking with him the livestock Georgia had received as payment for her work.

Georgia survived her failed marriage and was determined to never again get involved with anyone who expected her to make concessions with her career. Her devotion at that point was solely on her beloved dogs and her practice.

In 1910, Doctor Arbuckle Fix converted an old barn into a sanitarium. It was a place where patients could undergo physical or spiritual treatment and stay as long as they wanted. One of the first patients was a cowhand struggling with a toothache. Georgia was awakened late at night by the urgent cry of a man in great pain. He couldn't wait for the itinerant dentist to make his way to town and pleaded with Georgia to remove the offensive tooth. She reluctantly agreed.

The cowboy took his place in one of Doctor Arbuckle Fix's chairs and she instructed him to grab the arms tightly and keep still. She then ordered the man's friend to hold his head in place. Once everything was in order, she began the procedure. The man wriggled and screamed as the doctor tried to coax the tooth out of his mouth with a pair of crude forceps. The man's legs buckled and the spurs on his boots raked across the doctor's foot. She yelped. "Watch it there," she warned. "I'm not a bronco, you know." Georgia went on with her work and after several more minutes, the tooth finally broke free.

Doctor Fix's generosity extended beyond the medical care she gave her patients. She opened her home to women teachers in the area who had no place to live and to civic organizations that had no place to meet. Missionary societies, benevolent groups, drama clubs, and library clubs gathered in her front room to plan fundraisers and special events. As an advocate of health education, she donated her time to help teach at various county schools and even donated a microscope for students to study germs and fungi.

Georgia's home and sanitarium were warm, inviting locations where animals, as well as humans, were made to feel welcome. Along with a few dogs, cats, and goats, a variety of birds resided with Doctor Arbuckle Fix. At one time she had thirty-three canaries, a parrot, and an owl. Children who proved they could care for a pet were given one of her birds as a present. Friends and associates boasted that she was "truly gracious to all creatures."

After a particularly rough and wet house call trip in 1916, Doctor Fix developed a bad cold that left her an asthmatic. Frequent trips to the dry California climate brought her some relief, but not enough to sustain her life. She eventually died from the breathing condition on July 26, 1918, in San Diego, at the age of sixty-eight. Those with her at the end stated her last words were from the book of Psalms.

Doctor Fix's body was brought back to Nebraska and she was buried near her home in Gering. Many local citizens attended her service. She was remembered as someone who "went about doing good." Even in death she proved that statement to be true. She left her life savings to the community, to build a home for the needy. The inscription on her tombstone at the West Lawn Cemetery reads: IN MEMORY OF DOCTOR GEORGIA A. FIX, PIONEER PHYSICIAN. SHE PASSED AWAY IN 1918 AFTER THIRTY-TWO YEARS OF FAITHFUL SERVICE IN THE NORTH PLATTE VALLEY.

# SUSAN LA FLESCHE PICOTTE

FIRST FEMALE NATIVE-AMERICAN PHYSICIAN

*I have lived right with them for over twenty years practicing
medicine, attending the sick, helping them with all their financial
and domestic business and anything that concerned their personal
family life.*

—Dr. Susan La Flesche Picotte, 1914

Twelve-year-old Susan La Flesche wiped the perspiration off the
brow of an elderly Omaha Indian woman stretched out on a cot
before her. The woman's sad eyes found Susan's, and she lifted her
feeble hand out for the girl to take. Susan helped the frail patient
raise her head and take a sip of broth. Almost as if the effort had
been overwhelming to her delicate frame, the ailing Native
American fainted. Susan gently laid the woman's head onto a pillow
and dabbed her warm cheeks with a cool cloth.

The light from a gigantic moon streamed through the open
flap of the buckskin tepee situated on the Omaha reservation near
Macy, Nebraska. Susan left the sick woman for a moment to peer
out into the night. She lingered a bit and listened to the sounds of
the evening. With the exception of the cries of the coyotes in the
far distance, all was quiet. It was late, and the elderly woman's
breathing was labored. A messenger had been sent out four times
to get help, but the physician, hired by the government to care for

19

AT THE AGE OF TWELVE, SUSAN LA FLESCHE
BEGAN TO IMAGINE HERSELF AS A DOCTOR, AND BY THE
TIME SHE WAS TWENTY-FOUR SHE HAD BECOME THE FIRST
FEMALE NATIVE-AMERICAN PHYSICIAN.

sick and dying Omaha Indians, would not come. He was hunting prairie chickens and could not be persuaded to visit the reservation. It was 1877, and the health of an Indian woman was inconsequential to the white reservation doctor.

Susan spent the remainder of the evening hopelessly trying to make the woman comfortable. The agony of the lady's unknown affliction continued until the morning. By the time the sun had fully risen, the woman had passed away. Susan stood over the lifeless body, contemplating the tragedy and deciding her own course of action. If she were a doctor, she would respond quickly to Indians in need of medical attention. Their lives would matter to her.

Such were the circumstances surrounding Susan's initial interest in medicine. After witnessing the old woman's agony, she resolved to "serve others, visit the poor, and help the suffering humanity."

Susan La Flesche was born in June of 1865, the youngest daughter of Omaha Indian Chief Joseph La Flesche and his wife, Mary. Susan, her three older sisters, and two brothers were raised to generously give of themselves to those in need.

At the insistence of her parents, and like her siblings before her, Susan took full advantage of the "white education" offered to children on the reservation. The focus of the white missionaries who ran the school was to transform the seemingly wild Indian into a respectable citizen of the United States. Susan would allow them to teach her new ways, but would never fully abandon the traditions in which she was raised. According to Susan's journal, "the old ways are not devoid of values, culture, and emotional ties, and need always to be preserved."

Chief La Flesche instilled many values in Susan and her brothers and sisters. He was a farmer, and his children worked alongside him as they grew up. Susan's jobs varied throughout the seasons. In the spring she sowed corn, hoed potatoes, and weeded. In the fall she lent a hand with the harvest. Throughout the year she foraged wood, tended to the livestock, dressed animal skins, dried bison meat, and carried water to the camp from a nearby stream. With few exceptions Susan's childhood was idyllic. The United States government's attempt to rid the Omaha people of their "Indianness" was the only major difficulty she faced in her younger years.

Susan excelled in school and was often hailed by her teachers as an "exceptional student with massive potential." At the age of fourteen, with her eyes fixed on a career in medicine, Susan persuaded her parents to allow her to further her learning at the Elizabeth Institute for Young Ladies in New Jersey. Susan's sister had attended the school some years prior and was now a teacher on the reservation. Believing Susan would receive a better education at the institute, Joseph agreed to let her go.

Susan remained at the school for two and a half years. In addition to courses in English, Latin, literature, and music, she took on a number of college preparatory classes. The time she spent at the institute gave her a cross-cultural understanding that further enhanced her education. She returned to the reservation in 1882, a well-rounded seventeen-year-old with a greater knowledge of the government and the people seeking control of the Omaha Nation. Her goal now was to not only become a physician, but to be an advocate of Indian rights. Susan would learn from her father how best to politically serve the Omaha people.

Under Chief Joseph's leadership, the tribe was negotiating with Congress to remain on their ancestral homeland. Joseph needed the support of his well-educated children to help him through the process. Eventually, a land allotment agreement between the United States government and Native Americans temporarily halted the Omaha Indians from being pushed out of the territory. It would prove to be a short-lived victory. Susan celebrated the triumph with her family, unaware of the extent to which politicians would attempt to Americanize the Indians.

When Susan wasn't at home with her parents, she was working at the school on the reservation. The Presbyterian missionaries who ran the facility made a huge impression on her life. She wholeheartedly embraced their religion and accepted a position as a teaching assistant.

Susan enjoyed the experience, but her ambition did not lie in teaching. She left the school six months into the first semester and took a job as a nurse for an ill ethnologist. The woman was bedridden and suffering with inflammatory rheumatism. After five weeks Susan had helped restore the scientist's health. The woman was so grateful for Susan's efforts she provided partial funding for her to attend a school in Virginia and then to continue on to the Women's Medical School in Philadelphia.

In the fall of 1883, Susan once again left her family and tribe. Before she left, she promised her people that she would return and work among them as their physician.

A note in her journal capsulated her thoughts on the journey she was about to make: "I will come from the tepee to civilization."

Susan encountered people from all walks of life at the Hampton Institute in Virginia. She shared a variety of classes such as philosophy, piano, and art, with fellow Native Americans and black, ex-slave students from across the country. Her extracurricular activities included skating, playing tennis, and working with the Lend-A-Hand Club. The club collected gifts for the poor, visited the sick, and taught Sunday school.

Susan's daily routine began at 5:30 A.M. After chores and calisthenics, she would dress in a dark calico and muslin uniform, have breakfast in the cafeteria, and report to class by 9:00 A.M. Her studies continued until the evening meal was served at 6:00 P.M. Prayers in the chapel followed the meal, after which Susan would study until bedtime at 9:30. During the summer months, Susan taught school to underclassmen. The Federal Government strongly encouraged Indian women who wanted a career to consider teaching. But Susan had other plans.

A few months before graduating from the Institute, she applied and received acceptance into the Women's Medical College in Pennsylvania. Before making the trip to Philadelphia, she recalled the encouraging words of her father to her and her sisters when they were growing up:

*My dear young daughters, do you always want to be simply called those Indians or do you want to go to school and be somebody in the world? From that moment I determined to make something useful of my life.*

Susan's decision to enter the field of medicine met with opposition from the public at large. They found it unseemly that women should be in the profession at all, and particularly objected to an Indian woman in medicine. Susan faced criticism from the Omaha people as well. Indian women could become healers, but only after menopause. Native Americans believed that women were a spiritual danger to the tribe if they practiced healing anytime prior to that.

Funding for Susan's college education came from the Women's National Indian Association (WNIA). Many government agencies were against financially supporting Indian women seeking a higher education. They felt Native-American women should return to the reservation and assume their traditional roles.

Those in favor of Indian women in medicine, like the WNIA, argued that with medical knowledge and skills, Indian women could protect their homes, tribe, and families. Susan was in agreement with the WNIA, and when they asked for her thoughts on the matter, she expanded on their ideals:

> As a physician I will help the Omahas physically, teach them the importance of cleanliness, order, and ventilation, how to care for their bodies as well as care for their souls.

Susan entered the Women's Medical College in Philadelphia in October of 1886. The heavy course load for her first semester consisted of classes in chemistry, anatomy, obstetrics, and general medicine. In addition to her class work, she observed clinical practice at the women's hospital, took weekly examinations in all her subjects, and learned how to dissect the human body. Other women had trouble with dissections, but Susan did not mind the procedure:

> The students and I laugh and talk up there just as we do anywhere. Six students take one body . . . and [it] is divided into six parts. Two take the head . . . two the chest . . . two the abdomen and legs. Then we take off little by little. . . . It is interesting to get all the arteries and the branches. Everything has a name . . . from the little tiny holes to the bones. It is splendid.

Susan frequently sent letters home to her family in Nebraska, updating them on her studies. She bragged about the excellent teachers at the medical college and how fortunate she was to benefit from their wealth of knowledge. Surgeons often allowed medical students to watch them perform an operation, which provided Susan and the other students with a more in-depth way of learning.

After three years of hard work and examinations, Susan graduated. She was first in her class. When she accepted her medical diploma in August of 1889, she became the first Native American woman doctor in the United States.

It had been five years since Susan had left home, and she was anxious to return to Nebraska. Upon her arrival, she found her parents' health failing and the farm in disrepair. She immediately set to work bringing order to the homestead and treating her elderly mother and father. In an 1889 letter to a friend in Philadelphia, Susan wrote about her struggles and extolled the virtues of her western roots:

> *I can tell you one thing and that is a Western woman has to know how to do everything that a man does besides her own work, for she has to be ready for any emergency that may occur when men are not around.*

Throughout the summer Susan balanced household, field, and medical work. She cooked, sewed, measured land for a fence, pitched hay, harnessed horses, and, of course, nursed the sick. At the end of that long, hot season, a severe measles epidemic swept through the reservation, killing hundreds. Had the Omaha Indians trusted western medicine, Susan could have saved many of those lives. The tribe's people who did agree to be treated did so only after they witnessed Susan ingesting the medication herself.

The Indians lived miles away from one another, causing Susan to sometimes travel more than 25 miles between patients to make house calls. She was committed to the tribe and would go to great lengths to bring them medical care and any other assistance they needed. In 1889, she wrote:

> *If one wants to make a difference they must go out everyday. So much can be done by going to see them and while you are there tell them how to tidy up or show them how, which is better. These Omahas need help in many aspects of life . . . business, land, money, and horses, what kind to buy and all.*

Doctor La Flesche stood several inches shorter than most of her patients, but her medical capabilities made a tall impression. The vigilant care she gave members of the Omaha Nation instilled a sense of trust in the Indians, and her practice grew. Her reputation as a quality physician spread beyond the reservation, and, as a result, many whites as well as Native Americans sought her counsel. At one time she had a patient list of more than 1,200 people. "My office hours," she told her friends and family, "are any and all hours of the day and night."

In an average day, Doctor La Flesche's services to the public might include delivering a baby, stitching up a wound, negotiating business agreements between family members, writing a letter for an illiterate man, and paying a visit to bedridden patients on the far side of the reservation.

Once Susan's practice was well established, she began accepting speaking engagements at her former schools in both Virginia and Philadelphia, sharing her experiences as a doctor on the western plains with captivated audiences. Government officials in attendance were moved by her personal testimony and influence with the Omaha Nation. They encouraged the powers-that-be at the Office of Indian Affairs to appoint Susan as the chief physician to the government boarding schools for Native Americans. She accepted the post, and in a short time transformed the dismal sanitary conditions at the facilities into safe, hygienic environments.

No matter what offices Susan held in addition to that of doctor for the Omaha reservation, she remained most concerned about her fellow tribesmen. In 1890, a large percentage of the Omaha population was suffering from a highly contagious eye disease. Susan directed all her efforts to battling the epidemic. She isolated the infected patients from the rest of the tribe and instructed all of the Indians to use separate towels and washbasins. Lack of clean water made the road to recovery a long one, but eventually the tribe's health was restored. Doctor La Flesche's vigilance kept the death rate low during outbreaks of influenza and tuberculosis as well.

By 1892, Susan's hectic work schedule and the strain of caring for her ailing mother (her father had passed away in 1888) were taking a toll on her physical well-being. Since she had been a small girl, she had suffered with a painful and degenerative bone disease that affected her inner ear. The long hours she kept and the many miles she traveled to see patients exasperated the problem until she collapsed. After several months of bedrest, Susan went back to work, but it only temporarily. Her mother's declining health forced her to resign her position as reservation doctor so she could care for her full time.

For the first time in twelve years, Susan's focus was on bettering the health of two people as opposed to hundreds. Just as she was settling into a semi-retired lifestyle, she met a man and fell in love. Henry Picotte, a Sioux Indian from South Dakota, was a farmer and a divorced father of three. Historians report that Henry was a "handsome man with polite, ingratiating manners and a happy sense of humor." Susan and Henry were married on June 30, 1894.

The Picottes moved to a quaint house in Bancroft, Nebraska. Three weeks after they exchanged vows, Susan began seeing patients in a makeshift office in the living room of their home. Within a year of reopening her practice, she succumbed to the same illness that had plagued her earlier. Her condition was further complicated by the fact that she was now expecting her first child. In spite of her poor health, she managed to carry the baby to term. The birth left her physically weak, but her spirits were strong. Henry and Susan named their eight-pound son Caryl. "He has thick black hair, and his brilliant black eyes follow us all over the room," Susan wrote in her journal.

Once Susan was back on her feet, she returned to her medical practice. Caryl would play in the same room where she examined her patients, and he accompanied her on house calls as well. Susan noted in her journal that Henry was a supportive husband and would often take care of their son when she had to travel great distances to visit the sick.

In early 1898, the Picottes added another member to their family when Susan gave birth to another boy. They named this son Pierre. Despite the strain of motherhood, Susan continued practicing medicine.

Throughout the course of her lengthy career, Susan never lost sight of the main reason she initially entered the field of medicine. She remained dedicated to improving health conditions for the

Omaha people. When her practice first opened, she achieved that goal by tending to healthcare needs; later in her life, she strived to make things better by way of legislation.

Troubled by the increasing number of Indians who had become addicted to alcohol, she appealed to the Commissioner of Indian Affairs to help deal with the impact the disease was having on adults and children alike. In her 1900 letter to Commissioner William A. Jones, she wrote:

> For four years, from 1889 to 1893, I worked among the Omahas. . . . At first I went everywhere alone . . . and felt perfectly safe among my people. But intemperance increased until men, women, and children drank; men and women died from alcoholism, and little children were seen wandering the streets of the towns.

Susan explained to Commissioner Jones that men were using the money they earned from leasing their land to the government to buy liquor. "They only buy whisky," Susan wrote, "no machinery for their farms, no household improvements are made, and complete demoralization prevails."

In 1901 Doctor La Flesche Picotte made an impassioned plea for help to a grand jury in the fight against the sad toll whisky was having on the Omaha people. She cited many examples of Native Americans dying as a result of alcohol. "We are a very moral people," Susan insisted, "torn apart by the white man's poison." She urged the court to "take action before the tribe declined to nothing."

The issue of alcoholism was also a personal one for Susan. Her beloved Henry died in 1904, as a result of tuberculosis and heavy drinking. She demanded from politicians the vigorous prosecution of the law that prohibited the sale of liquor by both non-Indians and Indians on all reservations. Inadequate funding and a shortage of enforcement officials, however, made that next to impossible to uphold.

In spite of the problems, Susan stood firm in her crusade against "spirited drink." By 1907, Susan could finally see the results of the attention she and others had brought to the issue of excessive drinking. In a follow-up letter to the Commissioner of Indian Affairs, she wrote that the Omaha people "were drinking much less, working better, and beginning to get interested in church."

When Doctor Susan La Flesche Picotte wasn't acting as a spokesperson for the Omahas and working for the economic, social, and spiritual advancement of Native Americans, she was serving on various medical boards in the area and was the health inspector for the reservation schools. She also helped raise money to build a hospital on the reservation. On January 10, 1913, construction on the Omaha hospital was complete. A dedication ceremony was held and Susan was credited for making the dream of such a facility a reality.

By the end of 1913, Susan's health was again questionable. The surgery she had the previous year to help alleviate the pain in her ears had left her with a paralysis of facial muscles and a "nervous condition." She was later diagnosed with bone cancer and underwent a series of operations to remove the infected areas.

Doctor La Flesche Picotte died on September 18, 1916, at the age of fifty. The *Times* newspaper in Walthill, Nebraska, reported that "her life was dedicated to their [Indian] needs . . . to the furtherance of . . . their personal and collective welfare . . . as she always gave willingly to her people."

The hospital Susan helped build was declared a national landmark in 1993. It is now a community center. A plaque outside the facility commemorates Susan's accomplishments and simply reads: DOCTOR LA FLESCHE PICOTTE, THE FIRST WOMAN PHYSICIAN AMONG HER PEOPLE.

# SUSAN ANDERSON

## COLORADO HEALER

*I came here (Colorado) to die, but since I didn't get the job done, I guess I'll just have to live here instead.*

—Doctor Susan Anderson, 1907

A dazzling setting sun cast long shadows of birch and eucalyptus trees over the small cabin they surrounded near Fraser, Colorado. The home's sole occupant, Doctor Susan Anderson, admired the golden shafts of light streaming in through a half-opened window and onto the pages of the opened Bible in her lap. A light breeze washed over her delicate frame and she turned her attractive face into the wind. She brushed back her dark hair and closed her blue eyes for a moment. Doctor Anderson was tired. She had moved to Fraser in 1907 to rest and to try to overcome the tuberculosis that had assaulted her lungs. Although the recovery had been slow, she was now on the mend and longed to resume her medical practice.

Women doctors were not well received in western communities in the early nineteenth century. In the one-year period Susan Anderson had lived in the quaint town, her services were called upon very few times and only when male doctors were unavailable.

The attention she gained after stitching up a rancher's injured horse had attracted some human clients, but not many. She was

**DOCTOR SUSAN ANDERSON STANDING AT HER COLORADO CABIN
WITH HER BROTHER AND FATHER**

confident that, given time, she could prove her value and grow her business. Meanwhile, she was content to drink in the fresh air and enjoy a peaceful evening.

A boy's voice in the near distance coaxed Doctor Anderson out of her comfortable chair and to the door. The frantic young man ran up the dirt road to the modest house, calling out the doctor's name with every step. As soon as he arrived, he blurted out news of a sick baby who needed Susan's help. He was sent to bring the "woman doctor" to the ailing infant, some fifteen minutes away. After learning that the town's male physicians were not able to attend to the child, Susan grabbed up her black leather bag and followed the lad back to town.

Doctor Anderson met her patient's worried parents at the train depot. The father hovered over his pregnant wife as she cradled their tiny one-year-old daughter in her arms. The doctor looked into the tear-filled eyes of the mother as the father pulled back the ragged blanket wrapped around the infant. The baby was extremely thin, her breathing was labored, and her eyelids were swollen. Although she had never seen such an advanced case, Susan was certain the child was suffering from scurvy a disease caused by a deficiency of Vitamin C.

The desperate couple, whose faces and hands wore the scars of years of laboring in the fields, watched Doctor Anderson examine their baby. She gently questioned them about the girl's age and what they had been feeding her. They told the doctor that the baby was breast-fed for a while, but was now on canned milk. The homesteaders believed that canned milk was an adequate substitute. Doctor Anderson knew better.

After checking the little girl's gums and listening to her heartbeat, Susan gently stroked the baby's face with the back of her hand. She hesitated a bit before shaking her head. She apologized and told the anxious parents that there was nothing she could do.

Doctor Anderson blinked away a tear, then turned her attention to the distraught mother. She instructed the woman on the importance of regularly eating fresh vegetables and fruit and warned the grieving father against working his wife so hard. She further told the pair to stay away from canned milk, advising them to feed any other babies they might have with mother's or goat's milk.

The baby whimpered and her sobbing mother tried to make her comfortable. Doctor Anderson demanded that the couple bring the child they were expecting to her after it was born. The father searched his ragged suit of clothing over for money. After a few minutes, he sadly turned his empty pockets out and hung his head in shame. Susan told him that money was unimportant in such matters. She promised to have them arrested if they didn't comply with her request, however. The pair agreed and left the depot to spend the last remaining hours of their baby's life at their home.

The life of a doctor in the Old West was a terrible one at times, but Susan had come to expect such difficulties. The journey from her childhood to becoming a doctor had been a trying one, but she had persevered and realized her calling to help preserve lives.

Susan was born on January 31, 1870, in Nevada Mills, Indiana. Her mother, Mayra Pile, was her earliest female influence. Kind-hearted and protective, Mayra encouraged her daughter to read and write at an early age. Susan's father, William H. Anderson, was a farmer. He would live out his dream of being a doctor through his daughter.

Susan's parents divorced in 1875 and shortly thereafter, William left the area with his daughter and two-year-old son. Susan and her brother, John, were brokenhearted about leaving their mother. For reasons unknown to the Anderson children, William wanted no part of Mayra, and forbid his son and daughter from interacting with her as well. The three moved to Wichita, Kansas, where William homesteaded a farm along with his mother, father, and brother.

In time the Anderson's Kansas farm was as successful as their homestead in Indiana. William not only had a knack for agriculture, but was also gifted in nursing hurt and sick animals back to health. It was a talent he passed on to Susan. William doted on his daughter and encouraged her to be well read and knowledgeable in a variety of subjects. One of the areas she excelled in was Morse code. In her early teens, she let her father know that she wanted to be a telegrapher. William discouraged the notion and suggested she set her sights higher. He was determined for her to become a doctor. Susan dutifully obeyed her father.

Not long after graduating from high school, Susan and her brother moved to Colorado with their father and his new wife. The Andersons arrived in Cripple Creek in 1892. William traded his interest in farming for a career in gold mining. Susan's focus remained on medicine, and in the summer of 1893 she enrolled as a medical student at the University of Michigan.

With the exception of one class, the limited number of female students at the Ann Arbor school attended most lectures with their male counterparts. The anatomy course, however, was segregated. The largely male faculty considered the separation of the sexes in such a setting appropriate.

In addition to keeping up with her daily studies, Susan took on an evening internship at a local hospital. Her schedule was brutal, allowing little if any time for sleep. She contracted tuberculosis from a patient of hers and developed a persistent cough that would stay with her the rest of her life. As her medical skills flourished, her health suffered. She graduated from medical school on June 5, 1897. Rather than take a position offered to her at the Women's Hospital in Philadelphia, she decided to move back to Colorado in hopes that the climate there would help her lungs.

When Susan viewed her graduation day pictures, she saw that they clearly showed the effects tuberculosis was having on her. In a letter to her brother, she alluded to her poor health, and how certain garments helped camouflage the dark shadows on her face.

*I have had some pictures taken. I will send you the proofs if I can find them. The ones in the black dress were taken first and I didn't like the dress so I put on a white waist and had them taken over. . . . The cheek hollow does not show so plain in it.*

Shortly after Doctor Anderson arrived in Cripple Creek, she decided to set up her own practice. The congested area already had fifty-five doctors and ten dentists, none of them female. Susan attracted many women to her office, helping them through illnesses men could not relate to. Her proficiency in cleaning wounds and staving off infections saved injured limbs from amputation and restored good health to women and men alike in the area. Her growing practice buoyed her spirits and kept the tuberculosis from worsening.

Doctor Anderson's health was further enhanced after she met the man of her dreams and they decided to marry. She felt a touch of her tuberculosis slip away as she happily made wedding plans. But the progress she was making quickly took a downward turn as a succession of unfortunate events invaded her life. On the day of the wedding, moments before the ceremony was to begin, Susan's fiancé left her at the altar.

While putting the pieces of her broken heart back together, she received news that her brother had come down with influenza. She rushed to be with him, but didn't make it in time. She made note of her tremendous loss in her journal:

*I came back to Cripple Creek to live again. Life seems so useless and in vain. No one now cares much whether I live or die. John was my best friend on earth and now my best friend is in heaven.*

In an effort to bring herself out of the depressed state she was in, Doctor Anderson decided to leave Cripple Creek and travel around Colorado. In the spring of 1901, she briefly settled down in Denver and opened an office, but her practice failed within six months due to the glut of physicians already established in the city. She then relocated to Greeley, a thriving farming community 54 miles away. Instead of going into business for herself again, she took a job as a nurse at the local hospital.

Susan's mental state improved while in Greeley, but her physical condition worsened. When a typhoid epidemic invaded the region, she decided to move and not risk her health. This time she settled in Fraser, Colorado. She rented a cabin and focused on nursing herself back to full health. She ate well, exercised, and rested. Her stamina increased, and in less than a year the consumption was in recession.

Susan's need for an income and the town's need for an additional doctor persuaded her to set up another office. Once Doctor Anderson had proven herself to the community, she was called on day and night.

In the winter of 1908, she was summoned to the bedside of a young man who was suffering from pneumonia. When she arrived on the scene, the ailing teenager was surrounded by his worried family. The boy was lying on a cot next to a lit stove, shivering under a mound of blankets. He had a bad cold and a high temperature. Doctor Anderson examined the patient and contemplated her course of action. The helpless but trusting look on the faces of the boy's parents and siblings prompted her to pursue an unusual treatment she believed would save his life.

She instructed the family members to fill washtubs with water and boil it. She needed clean blankets, several pitchers, and bowls.

Once all those items were made available, she pulled the covers off the sick boy, sat him in the tub of hot water, draped a blanket over his shoulders, and opened all the windows.

Over the next several hours, Doctor Anderson drenched the teenager with water from head to toe, telling him to breathe in the fresh air as she poured the pitchers and bowls of liquid over him. As he did so, she thumped on his chest, dislodging the phlegm built up in his lungs. Just before dawn, the boy's fever broke, and he was well on his way to a full recovery.

Many of Doctor Anderson's patients lived in forests, ranches, or lumber camps. The carriage ride to and from their homes could be long and boring. To pass the time as she made her way to the sick or injured, she would practice shooting targets with her .38 revolver. The gun she carried was for protection from thieves and mountain lion attacks.

Doctor Anderson's reputation as a physician spread throughout the country. With every passing year, more and more people depended upon her skills as a surgeon and general practitioner. She mended bullet wounds, set broken limbs, and even removed a few abscessed teeth. She traveled from homestead to homestead, looking in on new mothers and babies and giving lectures on nutrition. She seldom, if ever, took any monetary payment from the most needy of patients. She was so revered that loggers, whom she had nursed back to health, built a new house for her as a show of appreciation.

Doctor Anderson was so dedicated to the health and fitness of her patients that she risked her own well-being to respond to an emergency. When she was summoned to help injured rail workers in a nearby town, she fell into an engine pit while making her way to them. The fall left her with several bruises, burns, and broken ribs. She was rescued and taken to a friend's home to recuperate. After dressing her wounds, she requested a corset from her caretaker. She was then laced into the garment, which held her ribs firmly in place. Within a few weeks, she was back on her feet.

Doctor Anderson's reputation extended beyond rural areas. Members of the staff at Colorado General Hospital in Denver recognized that she was an exceptional healer, and the best diagnostician west of the divide. Her honest business practices and her notoriety in medicine prompted Grand County, Colorado, politicians to appoint her as coroner. She accepted the position during the time that construction was in process for a new tunnel that would run through a mountain pass. The tunnel would replace a treacherous road that was often left impassable by heavy rain and snow.

Doctor Anderson's job required that she care for injured construction workers and challenge the tunnel commission to make labor conditions safe. Susan held the commission responsible for the nineteen deaths that occurred and the hundreds of men who were hurt or who got sick and died during the construction of the tunnel. In an emergency Doctor Anderson would venture into the 6-mile tunnel to give first aid to hurt men and help retrieve dead bodies.

By 1925 Doctor Susan Anderson had spent thirty years working in medicine. Society was more tolerant of women doctors, but she still struggled against those who simply could not accept her in this nontraditional role. In an attempt to drive Susan from practicing medicine, some men staged embarrassing office calls. One particular afternoon a tunnel worker who had been drinking maneuvered an appointment with Susan. The slightly inebriated man pointed to his fly when describing the physical problem he was having. Doctor Anderson suggested he might feel more comfortable talking with a male physician, but he insisted he needed her help. On the off chance that the man had a legitimate complaint, Susan agreed to examine him.

After being asked a few cursory questions, the man dropped his pants down around his ankles and stood staring at Susan. Unimpressed and with complete composure, she asked him what the problem was. He smiled and said, "Nothing. But ain't it a dandy?" Susan calmly ordered the man to pull up his pants. As he did, she reached for a nearby scalpel. While he was reattaching his suspenders, she cocked her fist back and told him to get out of her office. She showed him the knife and his eyes widened. "If I ever see you again," she warned, "I'll slit your belly with a butcher's knife." Before the man left, she made him pay a $10 examination fee.

The story of the life, times, and trials of Doctor Anderson made its way to many newspapers and magazines. Readers were fascinated with the tenacity and drive of the female pioneer doctor. The celebrated actress Ethel Barrymore was among her biggest fans. She sought out and Susan offered to make a movie about her life. Susan repeatedly turned her down.

Doctor Anderson practiced medicine for more than fifty years. In 1958, at the age of eighty-eight, Susan was hospitalized and lived out the remainder of her days at Colorado General Hospital. She passed away on April 16, 1960 and was laid to rest near her brother John in the Mount Pisgah cemetery in Cripple Creek.

# NELLIE MATTIE MACKNIGHT

## BELOVED CALIFORNIA PHYSICIAN

*Taken as a whole they will probably never amount to much unless the experience of the past belies that of the future. While this is so, yet no person of extended views or liberal ideas can desire to see the doors of science closed against them.*

> —Doctor R. Beverly Cole (a prominent male physician) in a speech delivered to members of the California Medical Society, 1875

Eighteen-year-old Nellie Mattie MacKnight stepped confidently into the spacious dissecting room at San Francisco's Toland Hall Medical School. Thirty-five male students, stationed around cadavers spread out on rough board tables, turned to watch the bold young woman enter. The smell of decomposing corpses mixed with the tobacco smoke wafting from the pipes of several students assaulted Nellie's senses. Her knees weakened a bit as she strode over to her appointed area, carrying a stack of books and a soft, rawhide case filled with operating tools.

To her fellow students, Nellie was a delicate female with no business studying medicine. Determined to prove them wrong, she stood up straight, opened her copy of *Gray's Anatomy,* and removed the medical instruments from the case.

It was the spring of 1891. She nodded politely at the future

WATCHING HER CLOSEST FAMILY MEMBERS DIE FROM
TYPHOID FEVER BROUGHT NELLIE MACKNIGHT TO
THE MEDICAL PROFESSION.

doctors, who glowered at her in return. A tall, dapper, bespectacled professor stood at the front of the classroom, watching Nellie's every move. The sour look on his face showed his disdain for a woman's invasion into this masculine territory. "Do you expect to graduate in medicine or are you just playing around?" he snarled. The blood rushed to Nellie's face and she clenched her fists at her side. She had expected this kind of hostile reception when she enrolled, but was taken aback just the same. "I hope to graduate," she replied firmly. Disgusted and seeing that Nellie could not be intimidated, the professor turned around and began writing on the massive chalkboard behind him. The students quickly switched their attention from Nellie to their studies. Nellie grinned and whispered to herself, "I will graduate, and that's a promise."

Nellie was born to Olive and Smith MacKnight on December 15, 1873, in Petrolia, Pennsylvania. She was one of three children for the MacKnights. Their son and first daughter died shortly after they were born.

Olive was very protective of her surviving child, and Smith, a land surveyor by trade, constantly showered his "only little girl" with attention. According to her autobiography, Nellie's early years were happy ones. She was surrounded by the love and affection of her parents and numerous extended family members.

In 1878 Smith MacKnight contracted a case of gold fever that drove him to leave his wife and child and head west. Before he left, he sent Olive and Nellie to live with his parents in New York. He promised to send for the pair once he had found gold.

Olive was distraught over the move from their home and the prospect of being without her husband. It was a heartbreaking experience from which she never fully recovered.

By the time Smith's first letter from California arrived, five-year-old Nellie and her mother had settled into life on the MacKnight farm. The absence of Smith made Olive quiet, withdrawn, and despondent. Aside from the time spent with her daughter, she seemed content to be left alone. Nellie, on the other hand, was outgoing and cheerful. She was particularly close to her grandmother, whose character was much like her own. Grandmother MacKnight taught Nellie how to cook and quilt, and how to prepare homemade remedies for certain illnesses. Her grandfather and uncle taught her how to ride a horse and care for animals.

As Olive slipped further into depression, Nellie became more attached to her grandparents. A letter from Smith, announcing that he had purchased a mine with "great potential," momentarily lifted Olive's spirits and gave her hope that they might be together soon. Several days later, news that Olive and Nellie would have to wait for the mine to pay off before Smith sent for them left her devastated all over again. The dispirited woman cried herself to sleep nightly.

The stability Nellie had come to know at her grandparents' home ended abruptly one evening in October of 1880. Her grandmother contracted typhoid fever and died after a month of suffering with the illness. Nellie watched pallbearers carry her grandmother's wooden coffin into the cemetery. She wept bitterly, wishing there had been something she could have done to save her. The subsequent death of her favorite uncle, suffering from the same ailment, served as a catalyst for her interest in healing.

Fearing for the physical well-being of her daughter, Olive moved Nellie to her father's home in Madrid, Pennsylvania. Any hopes the two had that their circumstances would improve at their new location were dashed when Olive became sick and collapsed.

The high temperature from typhoid fever made Olive delirious. She didn't recognize her surroundings, her family, or her child, and she cried out constantly for her husband.

Olive recovered after several weeks, but the fever and the sadness of being separated from Smith had taken its toll. Her dark hair had turned gray and the dark hollows under her eyes were permanent fixtures.

Smith's mine in Bodie, California, had still not yielded any gold and he was unable to send any money home to support his family. In order to keep herself and Nellie fed and clothed, Olive took a job at the Warner Brothers Corset Factory. Nellie attended school and excelled in all her subjects, showing an early aptitude in medicine. She pored over books on health and the human body.

When Nellie wasn't studying, she spent time trying to lift her mother's melancholy spirit. Letters from Smith made Olive all the more anxious to see her husband again and even more broken-hearted about having to wait for that day to come.

She began using laudanum, a tincture of opium used as a drug, to ease the pains she had in her hands and neck. The pains in her joints were a lingering effect of the typhoid fever. Olive developed a dependence on the drug and one night overdosed. She left behind a note for her daughter that read, "Be a brave girl. Do not cry for Mamma." Smith was informed of his wife's death, and although he was sad about the loss, he continued working his claim.

The day after Olive was laid to rest, ten-year-old Nellie was sent back to New York to live with her father's brother and his wife. Nellie's uncle was kind and agreeable, but her aunt was not. She was resentful of Nellie being in the home and treated her badly. Nellie endured her aunt's verbal and physical abuse for two years until her mother's sister invited Nellie to live with her at her farm 4 miles away.

Nellie adapted nicely to the congenial atmosphere and learned a great deal from her aunt about primitive medicine. After a short time with her aunt, Nellie finally received word from her father. Smith was now living in Inyo County, California, and working as an assayer and surveyor. Nine years of searching for gold had turned up nothing. Smith decided to return to his original line of work and he wanted his daughter by his side.

Fourteen-year-old Nellie met her father on the train in Winnemucca, Nevada. Smith agreed to meet with her there and escort her the rest of the way to his home. Although his face was covered with a beard and his eyes looked older, Nellie knew her father when she saw him. Smith, however, did not instantly recognize his child. He wept tears of joy as she approached him. "You're so grown up!" he told her. Little time was spent before the pair took their seats to continue their journey. Father and daughter had a long way to travel before they reached Smith's cabin in Inyo County. As the train sped along the tracks, Nellie was in awe of the purple blossoming alfalfa that grew along the route and of the grandeur of the Sierra Mountains.

Nellie continued to be impressed with the sights and people she encountered during their two-day trip to the homestead in Bishop. Smith promised his daughter a happy life among the beauty and splendor of the California foothills. In an 1887 journal entry, Nellie recorded her thoughts about how exciting, gay, and carefree she found her new home to be:

*The streets of the town were like a country road, lined with tall poplars and spreading cottonwoods—quick growing trees*

*marked boundary lines and gave shelter to man and beast. Their*
*leaves were pieces of gold in the sunshine.*

After a brief stay at her father's ranch, Smith enrolled Nellie at the Inyo Academy. She would be not only studying at the school but living there as well. Smith spent a great deal of time on surveying trips and wanted Nellie to be in a safe place while he was gone. The Inyo Academy was home to many young men and women whose parents were ranchers and cattlemen from all over the country. Nellie thrived at the school, and once again excelled in every subject. Upon graduation, she was valedictorian of her class.

Smith insisted the now seventeen-year-old Nellie should go to college and continue her education. She was in favor of the idea and decided to pursue studies in literature. Smith promised to pay for her schooling only if she chose law or medicine as her point of interest. Nellie wrote:

> *If I wished an education I must abide by his decision. My*
> *only knowledge of the law was "the quality of mercy." My only pic-*
> *ture of a woman doctor was that of Doctor Mary Walker, dressed*
> *in men's clothes and endeavoring in every way to disguise the fact*
> *that she had been born a woman. That I should choose neither*
> *was unthinkable.*

As Nellie contemplated her decision, her thoughts settled on her grandmother's struggle with typhoid fever and her mother's fatal attempt to ease the physical pain she suffered. It didn't take Nellie long to come to the conclusion that her "calling" was in medicine.

Just prior to Nellie graduating from the Inyo Academy, her father remarried. Nellie's initial reaction to her stepmother was one of indifference, but as she got to know her she had a change of heart. She was an extremely kind woman and never failed to show Nellie love and compassion. She encouraged her stepdaughter in her future endeavors and cried for days when Nellie moved to San Francisco to attend medical school.

Smith accompanied his only child to the Bay Area and on to Toland Hall Medical College. He paid her tuition, helped her find a place to live, wished her well, and returned to Bishop. Their parting was difficult. Nellie was grateful for the opportunity he was giving her and vowed to be home soon with a diploma in hand. Neither fully realized how difficult it would be to fulfill that promise.

The attitude of many of the Toland Hall professors and students toward women in medicine was vicious. Most felt a woman's presence in the medical profession was a joke. Nellie was aware of the prevailing attitude and was determined to prove them wrong. She devoted herself to her studies, arriving at school at dawn to work in the lab. She kept late hours, poring over *Gray's Anatomy* and memorizing the definitions of various medical terms.

The harder she worked, the more resentful her male classmates became. They exchanged vulgar jokes with one another whenever Nellie or one of the other two women attending the school was around, in hopes of breaking their spirits. Professors were cold and distant to the women, oftentimes refusing to answer their questions.

Doctor R. Beverly Cole, Toland Hall's Professor of Obstetrics and Gynecology, delighted in insulting female students during his lectures. He maintained publicly that "female doctors were failures." He told students, "It is a fact that there are six to eight ounces less brain matter in the female. Which shows how handicapped she is."

Nellie quietly tolerated Doctor Cole's remarks and allowed them only to spur her on toward her goal of acquiring a degree.

While in her third year of medical school, Nellie took an intern position at a children's hospital. Many of the patients that allowed her to care for them were Chinese. She assisted in many minor operations and births, and she helped introduce modern medicines and cures.

Months before Nellie was to graduate, she was granted permission to assist in a major surgery. Two physicians were required to perform an emergency mastoid operation on a deathly ill dock-worker. Nellie was one of two interns on duty and the only woman. The male intern fainted at the sight of the first incision. Nellie was a bit uneasy as well, but assured the doctor she could do the job when he ordered her at his side. She recounted the event in an 1893 journal entry:

> The surgeon talked as he worked. He described the blood supply, the nerve supply, the vessels that must be avoided, the paralysis that would follow if he invaded the sacred precinct of the facial nerve. Chip by chip he removed the bone cells, but the gruesome spectacle had been magically transformed into a thrilling adventure. I forgot that I had a stomach; forgot everything but the miracle that was being performed before my eyes, until the last stitches were placed, the last dressings applied.

Nellie eagerly looked forward to graduation day. In spite of the fact that her grades were good and her talent for medicine was evident, the male faculty and students remained unimpressed with her efforts. She was confident that when she and the two other female students accepted their diploma, the men would be forced to recognize that a woman's place in the emerging profession was a definite.

Shortly after passing her final examination, Nellie was summoned to the dean's office. The dean was a man who did not share Nellie's vision of women in medicine and because of that, she feared he was going to keep her from graduating. The matter he wanted to discuss, however, was how she wanted her name to appear on her diploma. She told the dean that her christened name would be fine. The man was furious. "Nellie Mattie MacKnight?" he asked her, annoyed. "Nellie Mattie?" Nellie did not know how to respond. "How do women ever expect to get any place in medicine when they are labeled with pet names?" he added.

The dean persuaded Nellie to select a more suitable name. She searched her mind for names from which her name might have been derived. "I had an Aunt Helen . . . and there was Helen of Troy," she thought aloud. "You may write Helen M. MacKnight," she said, after a moment of contemplation. The dean informed her that he would make the necessary arrangements. Before she left his office, he added, "See that it is Helen M. MacKnight on your shingle too!"

Nellie graduated with honors from Toland Hall Medical School. Her father and stepmother were on hand to witness the momentous occasion. As her name was read and the parchment roll was placed in her hands, she thought of her mother and grandmother, and pledged to help cure the sick. Chances for women to serve the public in that capacity were limited, however. Widely circulated medical journals stating how "doubtful it was that women could accomplish any good in medicine" kept women doctors from being hired. They criticized women for wanting to "leave their position as a wife and mother," and warned the public of the physical problems that would keep women from being professionals. An 1895 *Pacific Medical Journal* article surmised:

> *Obviously there are many vocations in life which women cannot follow; more than this there are many psychological phenomena connected with ovulation, menstruation and parturition which preclude service in various directions. One of those directions is medicine.*

In San Francisco in 1893, there was only one hospital where women physicians practiced medicine. The Pacific Dispensary for Women and Children was founded by three female doctors in 1875. The facility was designed to provide internships for women graduates in medicine and training for women in nursing and similar professions. Nellie joined the Pacific Dispensary staff, adding her name to the extensive list of women doctors already working there from all over the world.

In the beginning, Doctor MacKnight's duties were to make patient rounds and keep up the medical charts by recording temperatures, pulses, and respiration. After a short time she went on to deal primarily with children suffering from tuberculosis. She also assisted in surgeries and obstetrics, and was involved in diphtheria research.

In 1895, Nellie left the hospital and returned home to help take care of her ill stepmother. Within a month after Nellie's arrival, her stepmother was on her way to a full recovery. Nellie decided to stay on in Bishop and set up her own practice.

The response she received from the community and the two other male physicians in town was all too familiar to her. She persevered, however. She set up an office in the front room of her house, stocked a medicine cabinet with the necessary supplies, and proudly hung out a shingle that read HELEN M. MACKNIGHT, M.D., PHYSICIAN AND SURGEON.

Doctor MacKnight traveled by cart to the homes of the handful of patients who sought her services. She stitched up knife wounds, dressed severe burns, and helped deliver babies. As news of her healing talents spread, her clientele increased. Soon she was summoned to mining camps around the area to treat typhoid patients. Although her diploma and shingle read Helen M. MacKnight, friends and neighbors who had known her for years called her "Doctor Nellie." It became a name the whole countryside knew and trusted.

While tending to a patient in Silver Peak, Nevada, Nellie met a fellow doctor named Guy Doyle. The physicians conferred on a case involving a young expectant teenager. Doctor Doyle treated Doctor MacKnight with respect and kindness. Nellie was surprised by his behavior, and made note of her reaction in an 1898 journal entry:

> *I had worked so long, fighting my way against the criticism and scorn of the other physicians of the town, that it seemed a wonderful thing to find a man who believed in me and was willing to work with me to the common end of the greatest good to the patient.*

What began as a professional relationship grew quickly into romance. The couple decided to pool their resources and go into business together. They opened an office inside a drugstore on the main street of Bishop. In June of 1898, Helen and Guy exchanged vows in a ceremony that was attended by a select few in Inyo County. According to Nellie's account of the event:

> *My wedding dress was a crisp, white organdy, with a ruffled, gored skirt that touched the floor all the way around. The waist had a high collar and long sleeves. The wedding bouquet was a bunch of fragrant jasmine. . . . A small group of friends came to witness the ceremony, and the gold band that plighted our troth was slipped over my finger.*

Doctor Nellie MacKnight Doyle and Doctor Guy Doyle provided the county with quality medical care for more than twenty years. The couple grew their practice and took care of generations of Bishop residents. Nellie and Guy had two children—a girl and a boy. The daughter followed in her mother's footsteps and pursued a medical degree. Upon her graduation from college, she was given a foreign fellowship in bacteriology.

Doctor Nellie M. MacKnight spent the last thirty years of her life studying and practicing anesthesiology. She died in San Francisco in 1957 at the age of eighty-four.

# PATTY BARTLETT SESSIONS

## MORMON PHYSICIAN

*A doctor, if he had good sense would not wish to visit women in childbirth. And if a woman had good sense she would not wish a man to doctor them on such an occasion.*

—Brigham Young, December 1851

The shrill cry of a woman in immense pain filled the otherwise quiet night sky over Utah's Salt Lake Valley. Patty Bartlett Sessions smiled down at the expectant mother and wiped the sweat off her forehead. Barely out of her teens, the woman was in the final stages of delivery and frightened of the experience her body was going through. Her pleading eyes found compassion in the fifty-two-year-old midwife caring for her.

Patty Bartlett Sessions had helped bring hundreds of babies into the world. The sparsely populated western frontier of the 1800s was in need of trained birth attendants who could help ensure mother and child survived the grueling process of labor and delivery. The gifted midwife calmly reassured the frantic mother-to-be with stories of the healthy infants she had laid in the arms of anxious mothers. The exhausted woman nodded and tried to smile through a contraction.

Patty did not solely rely on practical experience to help her with her job. She studied the pages of a medical book entitled

ONE TIME HELPING TO DELIVER A CHILD LED PATTY BARTLETT
SESSIONS TO PURSUE A MEDICAL PROFESSION.

*Aristotle's Wisdom: Directions for Midwives.* The publication contained
advice and counsel for delivering a baby, along with more than 300
photographs of fetuses in various stages of development. She had
pored over numerous books on the subject, and in 1847 was one of
the most trusted women in the midwife profession.

On Sunday, September 26, 1847, Patty assisted in the birth of the first male born in the Salt Lake Valley. Her role in the momentous occasion was predicted long before the boy was born. Her journal entry for that day does not tell who predicted the event, but the midwife was honored to be a part of history:

> *It was said to me more than five months ago that my hands should be the first to handle the first born son in the place of rest for the saints even in the city of our God. I have come more than one thousand miles to do it since it was spoken.*

Patty Bartlett Sessions's journey began thousands of miles from Utah in the small New England town of Newry, Maine. She was born on February 4, 1795, to Enoch and Anna Bartlett, and was the first of nine children the couple had together.

Like all her brothers and sisters, Patty was raised on the family farm and was required to do a variety of chores. She excelled in spinning, weaving, and sewing. The intricate stitching she used on her samplers would come in handy with stitching of another kind once she entered the medical profession. Although her mother and father did not require their daughters to attend school, Patty sought out an education. She learned to read and write from the Newry schoolmistress and was a gifted math student.

On June 28, 1812, Patty married a farmer named David Sessions. The newlyweds moved in with his parents in the nearby town of Ketchum. David's mother, Rachel, suffered from rheumatism and required constant care. While David tended to the crops, Patty tended to her mother-in-law. The daunting responsibility inadvertently led the teenager to pursue a career as a midwife.

Before Rachel had become disabled, she was the trained

attendant who neighbors and friends sought help from with obstetrical cases. One afternoon she received a frantic summons to the bedside of an expectant mother who was very ill. Physically unable to get to the mother-to-be quickly, Rachel decided to send Patty to lend a hand. She reassured her daughter-in-law that she had the compassion and common sense necessary to be of help, and Patty agreed to go.

When she arrived on the scene, the expectant mother was in labor and very sick. Patty thought the woman was dying. What she lacked in practical knowledge, she made up for in nerve and courage. Patty's presence and calming attitude comforted the distressed woman. She took charge of the situation, ordering the expectant mother to breath easily through the contractions.

By the time the doctor arrived, the baby had been born, and mother and child were resting comfortably. The pair were thoroughly examined and given clean bills of health. Patty was commended by the physician for a job well done and encouraged to enter the business. He told her the need for her skills was in great demand and promised that she would prosper in the profession.

Patty was intrigued with the prospect, but it wasn't until she experienced the thrill of helping to deliver another child that she decided to become a midwife.

Her education in the field would be well rounded. She studied obstetrics under Doctor Timothy Carter, a physician in Bethel, Maine; she learned about natural herb remedies from Native Americans; and she interned with elderly midwives in the area. Patty Bartlett Sessions devoted herself to learning all she could about natural labor and prenatal care. She earned a reputation as one of the best practitioners of her kind in the territory.

When Patty wasn't helping to deliver babies, she and her husband were working the land on their 200-acre homestead. With dedication and hard work, they grew their farm to include a large house, two large barns, several sheds, a sawmill, and a gristmill. Over the course of their twenty-five-year marriage, the couple had eight children. Only three of their children lived to adulthood. Typhus fever swept through the area, claiming the lives of two of the Sessions children and countless other residents in the small farming community.

Patty dealt with the loss as best she could while continuing to serve the town as midwife. David struggled to come to terms with the death of his offspring and sunk into a deep depression. The pair's spirits never fully recovered.

In 1833, a group of Mormon missionaries made their camp near the Sessions home and began ministering to them.

Their message changed Patty and David's life and brought them out of the deep pit of despair. Close to a year later, the husband and wife adopted the Mormon religion and were baptized into the faith. At the urging of the church leaders, David moved his family from Maine to Kirkland, Ohio. Patty's services continued to be greatly required. In addition to performing her daily household duties, she attended to numerous obstetrical cases. Her journal contains several entries describing the events and their outcomes, such as this account from May of 1836:

> *Rode twelve miles last night, put Sister _____ to bed, fine boy, etc.. Rode six miles and put Sister _____ to bed with a pair of twins, difficult case, severe labor, but the Lord blessed us and we got through all right. Patients safe, etc.*

In 1842, the Mormon Church leaders again called upon the Sessions family to relocate. This time they were to go to Nauvoo, Illinois. While in Nauvoo, Patty and David met the town founder, Joseph Smith. Smith was also the president and prophet of the Church of Latter Day Saints. He was taken with Patty's medical ability and the role she played as caregiver for other migrating Mormons. In keeping with the religion's polygamist practice, Patty accepted a proposal of marriage from Joseph Smith. On March 9, 1842, the two exchanged vows.

Smith and the Mormon Church put Patty's skills to work, and she began teaching young wives about motherhood and the importance of a proper diet for themselves and their children. From 1842 to 1847, the accomplished midwife assisted in bringing hundreds of babies into the Mormon family. Patty continued to provide expert services to mothers after the church made a mass exodus from the Midwest to Utah.

Patty Bartlett Sessions Smith was forty-nine when she arrived in the Great Salt Lake Basin. Her medical duties expanded well beyond her initial training and duties as a midwife. Using a medical guide called *The Family Physician,* she now provided a wide variety of healthcare treatments to members of the congregation. Those whose health she had helped restore lovingly referred to her as "Doctor Patty."

The leaders of the Mormon Church wholeheartedly approved of Patty's title and work, and would later encourage other females to enter the profession. In January 1868, Brigham Young announced, "The time has come for women to come forth as doctors in these valleys." Patty adhered to the church's practice of healing the body using natural herbs and foliage. She served as an officer on the Council of Health, an organization that believed that the "Creator placed in most lands medicinal plants for the cure of all diseases incident to that climate." Patty was an expert at mixing natural concoctions that calmed the senses and eased a myriad of pains.

Throughout her life Patty maintained meticulous lists that included the activities of the Mormon Church as they made their way west, the families she assisted, the babies she helped bring into the world, the classes she taught, and the other healthcare tasks she performed from day to day. Archivists consider her on-the-spot chronicle of the Mormon trail experience and life in early Utah a great contribution to history.

After having lost both her husbands, Joseph in 1844 and David in 1850, Patty married for a third time. In March of 1852, she pledged her devotion to John Parry. John was the first leader of the Mormon Tabernacle Choir. They were married seventeen years before he passed away.

Patty's career as a midwife and healthcare provider crossed over several states and spanned seven decades. In that time she helped deliver close to 4,000 babies.

Doctor Patty died of natural causes on December 14, 1892, in Bountiful, Utah. A biographical sketch of her life, published in the Utah Journal on the day of her death, notes the legacy she left behind:

> She lived to see her 4th generation and has left two sons, thirty-three grandchildren, one hundred and thirty-seven great-grandchildren, and twenty-two great-great-grandchildren. Total posterity, two hundred and fourteen. She was ever a true and faithful Latter Day Saint, diligent and persevering, her whole soul, and all she possessed being devoted to the Church and the

*welfare of mankind. She has gone to her grave ripe in years, loved and respected by all who knew her.*

Doctor Patty is recognized by the Mormon Church as the "Mother of Mormon Midwifery."

# NELLIE POOLER CHAPMAN & LUCY HOBBS TAYLOR

## DENTAL PIONEERS

*If we ignore them and downplay their efforts they will be forced to abandon the idea of being part of medicine.*

—Doctor A. E. Regensburger, in his address to the California State Medical Society, regarding women as doctors and dentists, 1875

Frantic pounding on the front door of Nellie Pooler Chapman's home forced the petite woman out of a deep sleep, off of her bed, and onto her feet. She quickly lit a nearby candle, threw on her robe, and hurried to answer the desperate person knocking and calling out for help.

As soon as Nellie opened the door, a scruffy miner pushed his way inside. His left hand was holding his left cheek and tears were streaming down his face. "I've got to see the doc," he pleaded. Nellie left the door standing open as she brushed her mussed hair from her face. "The doctor isn't here," she informed the man. "He's in Nevada looking for silver." The miner groaned in pain and cried even harder. "You've got to help me," he insisted. "I've got a bad tooth and it's killing me." Nellie stared back wide-eyed at the suffering man. "I'm not a dentist," she told him. "I don't know how to remove a bad tooth."

The man drew in a quick breath and winced. He was in agony.

"You've watched him work, though," he reminded her. "You know what to do. Please," he begged. Nellie thought about it for a moment, then ushered the tormented patient into the dental office in the back of the house. "I'll try," she told him.

Nellie's introduction into the field of dentistry was dramatic, but it suited her. Prior to helping her husband with his busy practice, she had aspired to be a poet. After working as his assistant for some time, she realized her calling was in an area of medicine few women had sought to enter.

Nellie Elizabeth Pooler was born in Norridgewock, Maine, on May 9, 1847. Like many families of that time, the Poolers traveled west in search of a better life in the California Gold Fields. Arriving in the Gold Country in 1855, fourteen-year-old Nellie met and fell in love with forty-four-year-old dentist Allen Chapman. The pair married on March 24, 1861.

Doctor Allen Chapman established his practice in Nevada City, California, in 1856. Shortly after their wedding, Nellie began training as his assistant. Her duties included sterilizing the dental equipment, applying iodine and pain relievers to patients, and handing her husband the tools he needed to work.

Allen proved to be a wonderful teacher, sharing his knowledge of dentistry with his wife and encouraging her to acquire a license of her own. After eighteen years of marriage, the bulk of which was spent learning about dental health, Nellie decided to make it official. In 1879, she became the first licensed woman dentist in the West.

The Comstock strike in Nevada attracted many fortune-seekers to the hills around Virginia City. In 1865, Allen Chapman was one of the thousands who hurried to the new state to strike it rich. Not only was Allen a miner in Virginia City, but he ran a dental practice there as well. Confident that Nellie could handle the practice alone with the training that he had given here, Allen turned his attention to mining.

Allen divided his time between working his claim, running his office, and traveling to visit his wife and two children. Once Nellie received her license, she assumed full control of the growing California practice. She outfitted the office with her own equipment, which featured

DR. NELLIE POOLER CHAPMAN'S WEDDING PORTRAIT

*Courtesy of Debra Chapman-Luckinbill*

the best, most up-to-date products available.

Her patients made themselves comfortable in a grand red velvet chair, fitted with a porcelain bowl on a stand, an aspirator, and a holder for a crystal water glass. The drills she used were the most sophisticated on the market. It was powered by a treadle, which worked like a flywheel as it was pumped. A large wooden cabinet in the corner of the room held medieval-looking dental tools and leather-bound copies of *The Principles and Practice of Dental Surgery* and *Gray's Anatomy Descriptive and Surgical.*

As the only dentist in a wide range of northern California, Nellie's dental practice was in high demand. She was recognized by most in the community as a qualified doctor who always made her patients feel at ease. Nellie continued to practice dentistry until her death in 1906. She was fifty-nine when she passed away.

*Courtesy of Debra Chapman-Luckinbill*

DR. NELLIE POOLER CHAPMAN ATTENDS TO A PATIENT
IN THE DEN OF HER HOME.

While Nellie Pooler Chapman was carving out a place for herself in history as the first licensed dentist in the West, Lucy Hobbs Taylor was making a name for herself as the first woman in the world to earn a Doctorate of Dental Science degree.

Born on March 14, 1833, in Franklin County, New York, Lucy Beaman Hobbs's interest in medical studies began at an early age. Her mother and father were killed when she was twelve years old. The ten children they left behind were forced to fend for themselves to stay alive. Although times were difficult, Lucy rarely missed a day of school, and helped support her family by working as a seamstress.

After graduating in 1849, she relocated to Michigan and took a job as a schoolteacher. Her desire was to become a doctor, but at the time, there was a very narrow range of occupations deemed socially acceptable for women. She decided to remain in the more traditional role of teacher until she could afford to challenge the world's conventional view of working women, and until she had enough money to apply to medical college.

In 1859, she sought admission to the Eclectic College of Medicine in Cincinnati, but was denied entrance because of her gender. Struck by her tenacity and drive, one of the professors at the college offered to give her private lessons in general medicine. At his suggestion she entered the field of dentistry.

Dental schools required students to serve two years as an apprentice with a licensed dentist before entering college. Lucy struggled to find a doctor of dental science who would grant her the opportunity to learn from him. Doctor Jonathan Taft, the dean of the Ohio College of Dental Surgery, permitted her to work in his practice while she continued her search for a place to apprentice.

After a year-long search, a graduate of the school offered her an apprenticeship. Upon completion of her private studies, she applied to Doctor Taft's alma mater. Once again she was turned down because she was a woman.

Rejection only made Lucy that much more determined to pursue her goal. The long hours she had invested poring over medical books and the practical experience she had gained at Doctor Taft's office, pulling teeth and making dentures, made her confident that she could do the job. With nothing more than drive and belief in her abilities, she decided to open her own practice. At the age of twenty-eight, she hung out her own shingle in Cincinnati. From 1861 to 1865, Lucy had dental practices in Ohio

ALTHOUGH SHE WAS AT FIRST REJECTED FROM DENTAL SCHOOL,
LUCY HOBBS TAYLOR SUCCESSFULLY BECAME THE FIRST WOMAN TO
RECEIVE A DOCTORATE OF DENTAL SCIENCE.

and Iowa. She was known by the Native Americans in both locations as "the woman who pulls teeth."

Her reputation as a quality dentist spread throughout the Midwest. Her male counterparts respected her perseverance and dedication to the profession. She was so well liked by her peers that they made an appeal to the American Dentists Association to allow her to attend dental school.

In November of 1865, Lucy was admitted into the Ohio College of Dental Surgery. The five years she had spent in private practice and the experience she had acquired as an apprentice prior to that allowed her to enter the school as a senior. When Lucy graduated on February 21, 1866, she became the first woman to receive a Doctorate of Dental Science degree.

Not long after graduation, Doctor Lucy Hobbs moved to Illinois and opened another practice in Chicago. It was here that she met James W. Taylor, a Civil War veteran and railroad maintenance worker. The two fell madly in love, and in April of 1867 they were married in front of a few friends and family members. That same year, Lucy and James moved to the western town of Lawrence, Kansas, where James had a job working in the rail yards. Tired of the long hours and physical strain of manual labor, James sought out another profession. Lucy suggested dentistry and her husband agreed. James studied under his wife until he was able to get his license. Together, the Taylors had a large, successful practice.

In addition to her business, Lucy was involved in a number of political and civic causes. She served on the state dental society as well as school and library boards, and she campaigned for women's rights. Her efforts made it possible for many women to enter the field of dentistry. She cited the open-mindedness the new frontier possessed for allowing such progress to be made, and in 1892 wrote:

> *I am a New Yorker by birth, but I love my adopted country—*
> *the West. To it belongs the credit of making it possible for women*
> *to be recognized in the dental profession on equal terms with men.*

Doctor Lucy Hobbs Taylor retired from her practice in 1886, but remained active in her community until her death in October of 1910. She was seventy-seven years old.

# MARY CANAGA ROWLAND

## LEARNED PRACTITIONER

*My father always said his girls were just as smart as his boy, and my husband said I was as capable as any man . . . All these ideas made me believe in myself and made me think I could do something worthwhile in the world.*

—Mary Canaga Rowland, 1932

Two well-dressed men with pistols holstered to their sides crossed the dusty thoroughfare of Herndon, Kansas. Through the wavering heat and stabbing glare of sunlight, Doctor Mary Canaga Rowland watched the pair check to make sure their six-shooters were loaded. "This office is about to get busy," she said to herself as she watched the men square off against a couple of ranch hands standing in front of the telegraph office.

Mary couldn't hear what the men were saying, but she could tell they were arguing. The quarrel quickly turned violent. One of the ranch hands reared back to throw a punch, but was stopped dead in his tracks by a bullet. The second ranch hand was just as quickly gunned down. The gunmen fled, firing their pistols in the air as they rode off. One of the injured men was carted off to the hotel and the other was delivered to Doctor Rowland.

The doctor's patient was covered in blood and writhing in pain. Mary tore the faded blue shirt away from the wound so she could begin the examination. Once the saturated material was removed, she began soaking up the blood with strips of material. The bullet had gone through the man's forearm and struck his suspender buckle, leaving an egg-sized lump just below his heart.

As Mary started dressing the piercing, the ranch hand pulled his arm away from her. "You're a lady doctor," he said incredulously. Mary stared down at him and offered a partial smile. "I know what you're thinking," she said. "Every man to his trade, but every woman to the washtub, right?" The ranch hand merely groaned. "I could just let you bleed to death," Mary added. He could tell she was serious and didn't resist as she gently lifted his injured arm onto a fresh sheet.

After Mary finished dressing the man's wounds and treating him for shock, he drifted off to sleep. In time he made a full recovery, but he would forever be reluctant to admit that a "lady doctor" had patched him up. In spite of the challenges she knew lay ahead, Mary was determined to change society's prevailing sentiment that medicine was "indecent for women to know."

Mariam Ellen Canaga was the oldest of four children born to Elias and Ellen Canaga. She was born on June 29, 1873, at the Canaga farm in Red Willow, Nebraska. Mariam—or Mary, as her family called her—was a precocious child who acquired an early interest in medicine from her mother, who helped support the family by caring for expectant mothers. She would help deliver their babies and stay with them for a week afterward to do the cooking and cleaning. When Mary wasn't with Ellen on the job, she was busy with the many chores she had to do around the homestead. Unable to keep her mind on farm work, Mary would occasionally sneak away to look at the books on midwifery her mother had hidden from the children. The subject matter fascinated Mary and fanned the flames of knowledge.

According to biographical information acquired from the Nebraska Historical Society, Mary was an exceptional student and an avid reader. At times her constant reading irritated her mother. Ellen felt Mary needed to be working instead, but Mary could not be torn away from her books. As she noted in her memoir:

> *I made up my mind that I was going to get more learning than our country school offered. At 13 . . . it was my sole objective in life to read everything I could lay my hands on.*

By the age of sixteen, Mary had graduated from high school and had been given permission from her parents to further her education at a school in the nearby town of Indianola. She found a place to live where she could work for her room and board. During the three-month break in between terms, Mary taught school and prepared herself as much as she could for the day she could attend medical college.

During her time at the school in Indianola, Mary met a lawyer and teacher by the name of J. Walter Rowland. Walter was a widower with four children, and although he was a fine teacher, it was not his life's ambition. Like Mary, he too had an interest in medicine. Their common goal to become doctors sparked a friendship that quickly blossomed into romance.

Mary and Walter courted for five years. During that time both had decided to go forward with their pursuit to be doctors. Walter left for Missouri to attend the Kansas City Medical College. Mary took a job as a schoolteacher in nearby Goodland, Kansas, and provided Walter with funds to get him through school. He promised to do the same for her when the time came.

Shortly after Walter graduated, he and Mary decided to get married. The two exchanged vows on March 26, 1897, and then moved to Herndon, Kansas, where Walter established a medical practice.

A doctor's services in the growing midwestern territory were greatly needed. The nearest hospital was 300 miles away, and other physicians were far and few between. A myriad of patients visited Doctor Walter Rowland at the couple's home office at all hours of the day and night. Mary had not had any formal medical training at that time and could only act as Walter's nurse. She assisted him on house calls as well, helping with bandaging and dressing wounds and providing the moral support necessary to deal with difficult cases. Before settling down in the evenings, she studied his medical journals:

*It was a fortunate thing for me that I could bury myself in Doctor Rowland's medical books. I wanted to understand everything so that I might be of help to him. How wonderful to study the human body, its physical makeup, the why and where of each part and its function; to study how to tell one ailment from another, the best forms of treatment and how the baby develops in the mother.*

After the Rowlands had been in Herndon for a year, Walter suggested Mary enroll at a school in Topeka, Kansas. In the fall of 1898, Mary happily entered the institution to begin her first year of study. She described herself in her journal as "full of ambition to be taught" and "absorbed in learning about the human body."

Mary enjoyed the required medical courses of chemistry, anatomy, and pharmaceutical instruction, and because she'd had practical experience in each subject, she made excellent marks. She transferred in 1899 to the Women's Medical College of Kansas City, Missouri, and graduated school in 1901. She then returned to Herndon and joined her husband in his thriving practice.

One of the first cases she treated involved broken bones. The way some of the injuries occurred was shocking to the new doctor. A family sent a nine-year-old Bohemian boy out at four in the morning on a June morning to herd cattle. About ten in the morning he grew sleepy and the cattle were doing all right so he lay down to sleep in the deep rut of the road. It was shaded by grass. It was time to cut the wheat and some men drove along with a team hitched to a header box, but because the rut was deep and the grass long, they didn't see him lying there. The little fellow woke up as the horses were passing over him. He tried to get out, but a wheel caught him across the thigh and broke the bone; it also cut his head.

Her method for treating the hurt boy was just as unconventional as the accident that had brought him to her care. Although Mary followed the instructions given in her college book on minor surgery, Walter worried the patient's leg would not mend. Mary, however, was confident the procedure she used would work:

> The men called for me and I put the lad on a flat bed on his back. Then I ran adhesive tape down both sides of the broken leg and under the foot. I ran a bandage through the tape beneath his foot and to this I attached a flat iron for traction. This method is called Buck's Extension. When the femur breaks, the muscles pull the broken ends apart and they do not heal. With continuous pull, however, the muscles give way after a while and the leg straightens out.

Mary let the boy rest in that position for a few days. After eight weeks, the boy's leg had healed so completely that no one could detect it had been broken.

Once Mary felt her career as a doctor was on firm footing, she and Walter made plans to start a family. Both longed to have children of their own, and on April 25, 1902, the couple had a daughter. Mary named the baby Nellie:

> As soon as I heard her cry she was mine against the world, and as long as life should last. I love my husband and now I loved my baby. It seemed that life had given me everything that one could desire. My heart was full of joy. My cup was running over. Surely God had laid his hand on me to bless me.

Mary and Walter barely had a chance to enjoy their little girl when tragedy struck the family. In what authorities described as a senseless act of violence, Walter was struck down by a town merchant named George W. Dull. The two men had exchanged words in a heated argument that to this day remains a mystery. Dull hit Rowland over the head with a blunt object, killing him almost instantly.

Doctor Mary Rowland laid her husband to rest beside his first wife at the cemetery in Indianola. Her grief was overwhelming at times, but she knew she needed to see beyond it to concentrate on providing for her child. Less than a month after Walter's murder, Mary resumed her work as town physician.

Her schedule was hectic. She would see to patients and then hurry off to nurse her baby. A young girl helped her with housework duties, meals, and laundry.

The loss of Doctor Walter Rowland was keenly felt in Mary's

life as well as in the community. Male patients could not bring themselves to be seen by a woman physician and decided to live with their ailments rather than seek Mary's expertise. Until she could prove herself capable of saving lives, most men stayed away.

A true test of her medical skills came in June of 1902, when she was called on to help a woman in labor who was dying. Mary's fragile patient was a seventeen-year-old girl, eight months along and suffering from convulsions. The convulsions momentarily stopped after Mary gave the teenager a small dose of morphine that put her to sleep. When the young woman awoke the next morning and her convulsions started again, Doctor Rowland decided to dilate the uterus and take the baby.

> It sounds easy but the uterus has the strongest muscle in the body and it contracted on my hand like a vise. It was some time before I was able to bring down the baby's foot. When I had succeeded in bringing down both feet and legs, my hand and arm were paralyzed and I let an assistant finish delivering the baby. . . . After a while he said, "I can't get the head out." Then I instructed him to let the baby's legs straddle his arm and to slip his fingers in the baby's mouth. After doing this the baby flexed its chin on its chest and slipped right out.

The young woman's condition was questionable for a few hours, but Mary was able to nurse the weak new mother back to health. Mary's ability in such a crucial circumstance earned her the respect and confidence of the men who had stopped seeking medical attention.

Doctor Rowland's reputation as a "fine woman physician" soon spread throughout the territory. Although her practice was consistently busy, she did not make a large salary. Many people offered her food and handmade items, as opposed to hard currency, in exchange for her care. She worried a great deal about how she would be able to continue providing for her daughter.

Concern for her child's well-being and the desire for a companion's support prompted her to accept a marriage proposal from a local businessman. Mary first met August Kleint when he was working as the town butcher. He had since abandoned that job in favor of a profession in real estate. The couple had problems from the moment they exchanged vows in 1904. August was resentful of the time Mary spent away from home with her patients. They battled over the changes he wanted her to make. Mary called their union "the greatest mistake of her life." Within a year of their marriage, the couple separated. They were not officially divorced, however, until 1909.

Some time before the dissolution of Mary's second marriage, she decided to turn her attention almost solely to the study of medicine. She wanted to go back to school and learn more about the subject that had become her life. With Nellie in tow she traveled to Omaha, Nebraska, and enrolled at the Creighton University School of Medicine. On April 19, 1905, Doctor Mary Rowland received her second medical degree.

Once Doctor Rowland graduated from Creighton University, she and her daughter moved to Topeka. She opened another practice, but quickly grew tired of the blowing dust and wind that was so prevalent in Kansas. From there she relocated to Lebanon, Oregon, and for the third time in her career, she opened a medical office.

In the beginning, both communities were reluctant to accept her skills. After hanging her shingle out in Lebanon, she overheard people talking as they passed by the sign. "Doctor Mary Canaga Rowland, a woman doctor, well, well, well . . ." The first patient she saw in Oregon was not opposed to women doctors. In fact he sought her out for just that reason:

> *He was a little boy of ten or eleven. He came to me about half past eleven one night and woke me up to take care of his hurt finger. He had been in a bowling alley and a ball had hit his finger. He was crying and I asked him how he happened to come to me and he said, "Cause I know'd you're a woman and you'd be careful . . ."*

The cornerstone of Mary's practice was always family medicine. She did, however, seek out job opportunities in other areas of the field. Hoping to aid United States soldiers fighting in the Mexican-American War, she traveled to Portland to join the U.S. Army. It was 1916, and military officials scoffed at her efforts before informing her that the Army did not take women. "I didn't know the first thing about the organization of any army," she later wrote in her autobiography. "I was unaware that women were not part of any army." Mary's brazen attempt to enlist made the front pages of several Oregon newspapers.

At the age of forty, Doctor Rowland uprooted her life again to continue her study of medicine. She left eleven-year-old Nellie behind while she attended a post-graduate school in New York. She appreciated the chance to add to her education, but found being away from her daughter quite difficult. Many of her letters to Nellie expressed her sorrow over the time they were apart. On August 4, 1913, she wrote:

*My darling Baby, I am so homesick for you, dear, but you be a good girl and I'll be back as soon as I can. I am learning a lot of new things here at the school and the hospital. I will send you some stamps in this letter so you can write to me often. Don't forget Mamma and be a good girl. Write. A world of love for you, baby. Mamma.*

The absence from her child proved too great to bear. In four months' time, Mary was back home again with Nellie.

Doctor Rowland's career as a female physician in the West spanned more than sixty years. In addition to maintaining a number of medical practices, she also held a position as the chief physician for the Chemawa Federal Indian School in Salem, Oregon, from 1913 to 1927.

In 1935, Mary remarried and had a second child. She kept up with her new family while attending to her patients, who suffered from illnesses ranging from measles to tuberculosis. Doctor Rowland's life ended on August 1, 1966. She died from natural causes at her Salem home. She was ninety-three years of age.

# ELLIS REYNOLDS SHIPP

## CHILDREN'S DOCTOR

---◆◆×◆◆---

*The more I learn, the more understandingly I can say we are*
*beautifully and wonderfully made.*

—Ellis Shipp, February 3, 1876

The sick baby cradled in Ellis Shipp's arms was too weak to cry. She stared sadly up at her mother with eyes pleading for help. Ellis had none to give her suffering daughter. She had employed all of the remedies she knew to give to typhoid patients, but nothing had worked. The eight-month-old little girl languished with a fever and softly whimpered. Ellis could only hold her beloved Anna close and rock her tiny frame back and forth until at last she passed.

Ellis tearfully mourned the death of her "precious one," but believed the Lord had great purpose in taking the child. Anna was the second baby she had lost in five years. The tragedy sparked a desire in Ellis to pursue an education in medicine. She felt her calling was inspired by God, and dedicated her life to helping preserve the lives of other mothers' ailing children.

Doctor Ellis Reynolds Shipp was born in David County, Iowa, on January 20, 1847. She was the oldest of the five children her parents, William Fletcher Reynolds and Anna Hawley, brought into this world.

In 1852, William moved his family across the Great Plains to

THE DEATHS OF TWO CHILDREN IN FIVE YEARS DROVE
ELLIS REYNOLDS SHIPP TO THE FIELD OF MEDICINE.

Utah so he could continue his work with the Mormon Church. The headquarters of the church was located in the Salt Lake Basin. The Reynolds clan settled in Pleasant Grove, 20 miles south of Salt Lake.

According to Ellis's journal, the first ten years of her childhood was idyllic. Her religious parents showered Ellis and her siblings with affection and attention. The death of her mother in

1861 brought an abrupt halt to what Ellis referred to as "one endless day of sunshine," and she was thrust into the position of family caretaker—a role she would hold for more than a year.

In the fall of 1863, William Reynolds remarried. Ellis resented her new stepmother's intrusion, and her actions reflected her feelings. She was ashamed of her behavior at times and cited her youth and inexperience as reason for her unwise outbursts of anger. In spite of a difficult period of adjustment, Ellis boasted that her father was patient with her. He continually reassured her of his love for his children, and he was a constant source of encouragement for the Reynolds clan.

At the age of twelve, Ellis gazed upon a photograph of a handsome twenty-year-old man and bragged to her friends that she would one day marry the subject of the picture. Not long after making that bold claim, Ellis met the man in the photograph at a party. "He was of noble form and feature," she wrote in her journal. "But the principal attraction was the eyes." Milford Shipp was just as taken with Ellis, and shortly after being introduced, the two began courting. Just as their romance began to blossom, Milford was sent on a mission trip for the Mormon Church. The two did not see each other again for five years.

During their time apart, Ellis dedicated her life to following the ways of the Mormon religion. She learned all she could about the principles and disciplines of the denomination. Brigham Young, president of the church, met the devoted teenager at a service and was moved by her level of commitment to the faith. He invited Ellis to live at his Salt Lake home as one of his children and study the word of God there. Ellis graciously accepted.

Milford's life was as full as Ellis's. Not only was he sharing the church's values and teachings with spiritually hungry people at each of his mission stops, but his personal life was active as well. He had entered into a tumultuous marriage that ultimately ended in divorce.

After the dissolution of the marriage, Milford set out on another mission trip. He was to travel through the Mormon settlements across the plains and preach. When he passed through Iowa, he and Ellis were reintroduced. After hearing him speak from the pulpit, the notion that she was destined to marry Milford was reaffirmed.

Ellis and Milford's relationship was rekindled, and seven years after their first meeting, the pair were wed in a simple ceremony. Milford was twenty-seven and Ellis was nineteen. Prior to exchanging vows, Ellis prayed to be a faithful wife and sustaining companion for her "dear Milf." Their wedding was one of Ellis's happiest moments. According to her journal entry dated May 5, 1866:

> *The ensuing few hours are somewhat confused in my mind but I know that Brother H.C. Kimball pronounced us one—and I feel that it was not all ceremony, but that our hearts were united in an indissoluble tie that all the vicissitudes of time and sorrow could not sever or unlink.*

The Shipps' first home was a fully furnished adobe cottage, and the newlyweds felt their small house was perfect. Just as they were settling into married life, Milford joined a militia to help protect their home and the Mormon emigrants from hostile Indians.

The Native Americans had killed a number of sheepherders working in the hills and canyons. Milford was among several hundred troops directed to prevent any future attacks on southern Utah residents.

During Milford's short absence, Ellis tended her garden, made rugs and blankets for their home, pored over books on health and nutrition, and maintained a journal. When her husband returned he was greeted with news that they were expecting a baby. The first of their ten children was born early in 1867, and Ellis noted the occasion in her journal:

> *Our Father of Love Divine bestowed upon me His mortal child, the most gracious and sanctified gift within His storehouse of blessings. A beautiful son! A body without blemish, endowed with a sanctified spirit! My beautiful baby boy!*

After a short time set aside to enjoy wife and child, Milford returned to his missionary work. Ellis was sad to see him return to the field, but she was proud of his dedication to the Lord. Her journal describes the love and admiration she had for Milford. She often noted that her passion for him was "akin to worship." A letter from Milford, the man she believed had "no moral weakness," temporarily halted her praise.

Milford informed Ellis that he had succumbed to the full mandate of their religion with regards to marriage, and would soon be bringing home a new wife. Ellis was devastated at first. She believed that plural marriage was a divine command from God, but she hoped she could be Milford's "only noble aim and purpose." After a great deal of prayer, Ellis's heart softened to the idea of the new woman in her life and home. Her attitude was further changed with the news that she was expecting another child.

In 1875, Ellis and Milford celebrated nine years of marriage.

During that time the couple had five children. Two of those children died in infancy, and one died at the age of five. Also during that time, Milford married two more women, bringing the total number of wives to four.

Throughout Ellis's married life, she maintained a thirst for knowledge. She was an insatiable reader and would typically arise three hours before the rest of the family to study religious and secular textbooks. She shared her education with students at the ward school, where she taught a variety of practical subjects. Ellis's chief area of interest was always medicine. She felt it was the responsibility of every mother to fully know the laws of health. Her daily routine required that she rise at four in the morning so she could spend time reviewing medical journals. The busy details of a typical day for Ellis were recounted in an 1872 journal entry:

> *Last night I wrote down my work for today which is as follows: Rise at four in the morning, dress, make a fire, sweep, wash in cold water, comb my hair, clean my teeth. Write a few lines in my journal. Write a letter to Grandmother. Read a chapter in Doctor Gunn on health. Read few extracts from Johnson. Dress the children, make bed, sweep, dust and prepare my room for the breakfast table. Breakfast at nine. Sew on machine until three. Dinner hour. After dinner call on Sister Jones, who is sick. Wash and prepare the children for bed; from six till eight, knit or do some other light work. Review my actions for the day—offer my devotions to Heaven and retire at nine.*

Ellis's interest in medicine did not go unnoticed by her family. Milford and his other wives encouraged her to consider attending school to pursue a degree in the field. Although many university board members, instructors, and much of the population at the time frowned upon females in the medical profession, Mormon Church leaders supported women in their faith in such ventures. The idea of Ellis attending medical school had been brought up before, but separation from her family had kept her from committing:

> When the subject was broached to me, as being one to step out in this direction, I thought it would be what I would love and delight in . . . if this knowledge could be obtained here. But the thought of leaving home and loved ones overwhelmed me and swept from me even the possibility of making the attempt.

Spurred on by the memory of her three children who had died, Ellis eventually decided to brave being apart from her family to learn how she might save the lives of other infants struggling with illnesses. On November 10, 1875, Ellis boarded a train bound for Philadelphia to enroll at the Philadelphia Medical College. As she tearfully waved goodbye to her sons, she tried not to think about the fact that she would not see them again for two and a half years. Instead she focused on the opportunity to acquire further knowledge in medicine and "make her life useful upon the earth."

Ellis's new home in Philadelphia was a boarding house, owned and operated by members of the church. Six hours after she had arrived in the city, she was seated in one of the medical school's halls to hear her first lecture. Her homesickness subsided as she realized how much she had to learn and how eager she was to learn it.

By January of 1876, Ellis had become fully acclimated to her surroundings and happily overwhelmed with schoolwork. In addition to lectures and laboratory studies, Ellis observed doctors making their rounds in clinics. She learned about illnesses that primarily attacked children. She noted in her journal that it was work she felt her gender was particularly suited for:

> *The knowledge I'm gaining now will make me more careful and more observing of little ailments in my children and meet every unfavorable symptom as it may occur. Who has greater need of understanding the laws of life and health than a woman? Truly I think she is the only one to study medicine.*

A constant stream of letters from friends and relatives in Utah helped sustain Ellis through the long hours spent poring over textbooks, completing endless homework assignments, and taking grueling examinations. In her limited leisure time, she accompanied licensed doctors through hospitals and observed as they diagnosed and treated patients.

Some of the more serious cases—such as burn victims or children who had lost limbs due to accident and subsequent gangrene—stirred her emotions and left her discouraged. Overall, though, she enjoyed school and was grateful for the exposure to all ailments and their treatment. In an 1876 journal entry, her enthusiasm seemed boundless:

> *How much to learn! I feel overwhelmed with the multifarious intricacies of medical education. Truly the greatest study of mankind is man, both physically and mentally.*

No matter how busy Ellis stayed with class work and field assignments, a deep longing for her children and husband would overtake her at times. Some days she was too lonesome to keep up with her daily journal. She dragged her sorrowful and weary frame from lecture to lecture, believing in those moments the only thing that could get her through another day was the sight of her sons. Acute melancholy and the cold air in the lab where Ellis and other classmates practiced dissection contributed to a failure in her own health. Although she felt dissection was necessary for learning about the intricacies of the human body, she found the practice of mutilating the body disconcerting. As she grew accustomed to the practice, her health was restored and the horrifying dread of the work itself wore off:

> All disagreeable sensations are lost in wonder and admiration. Most truly man is the greatest work of God. Every bone, muscle, tendon, vein, artery, and nerve seem to me to bear the impress of divine intelligence.

In addition to the standard studies of anatomy, metabolic diseases, and digestion, Philadelphia Medical School students were required to attend courses on basic dentistry and the administration of pharmaceuticals. Ellis's regular second-year routine also included classes in chemistry, electric therapy, and her favorite subject, obstetrics:

> Attended a clinic at twelve o'clock, obstetrics by Doctor Cleveland. This to me is the most interesting part of my studies. To understand this and the diseases of children shall be my greatest object for the next two years. To be able to treat these conditions and diseases successfully, I think there could be no greater accomplishment in the medical line. At four o'clock Mrs. Pratt and I

*attended a lecture by Doctor Eliza Judson upon the "Management of Infancy." To express the varying emotions that I experienced during that interesting and eloquent lecture would be impossible. In addition to the competency of the lady herself, the subject, to me so all-important, thrilled every nerve center of my being.*

The more Ellis learned about how to care for children, the more inspired she became to share her knowledge with mothers everywhere. In her journal she emphasized the importance of women awakening to the responsibilities of motherhood and striving to be better educated in order to tend to their offspring.

Lectures given on ways to ensure the health of infants were of particular interest to Ellis. She could not help but reflect on how valuable these lessons would have been to the life of her own babies who had died at an early age. She took detailed class notes, tracing the expected development of a child from birth to twenty-four months. The notes were taken not only to help her future patients but for her own personal edification:

> *. . . no living creature so utterly powerless, instinct only prompts it to sleep, cry, and nurse. The head of the infant at birth is more fully developed at birth than other parts of the body owing to the greater amount of pure blood which goes to this part. . . . When it enters the world it should be immediately wrapped in warm flannel and if [it is] a strong, healthy child [it] can be bathed and dressed without delay. . . . How necessary it is for mothers to cultivate the purest, mildest and ennobling emotions through these acts, for her child will partake of every sensation of her being.*

Ellis Shipp's high marks proved she was an exceptional student. Combined with her commitment to curing children's diseases, her exemplary grades prompted Philadelphia hospital administrators to offer her a summer internship position. She reflected in her journal that her hands-on experience there afforded her a chance to gain knowledge that would have been impossible to obtain by simply reading.

In an attempt to complete her studies earlier than the required four-year term, Ellis decided to spend her summers in class rather than return home. On March 14, 1878, barely three years since she began medical school, Ellis graduated and was on her way back to Utah. Many changes had occurred during her absence. Her children had grown and her husband's other wives had added to the Shipp lineage.

Milford had changed as well. Unbeknownst to Ellis, Milford had been studying law at the same time she had been studying medicine. A few months prior to her graduation, Milford was admitted to the Salt Lake Bar.

Once she was settled at home, Ellis began the happy task of reacquainting herself with her children. She was not in a hurry to start her own practice, but she felt compelled to do so as more female patients were referred to her by the male physician in the vicinity. Her priority was to family first and medical work second.

Ellis's work expanded beyond hearth and home and caring for the ailing. In the late 1800s, she was selected to represent notable Utah women at the National Council of Women in Washington, D.C. While in attendance, she presented a paper on the care and training of children. Her talk was heard by such well-known female leaders as Susan B. Anthony, Elizabeth Stanton, and Clara Barton.

Doctor Ellis Shipp's specialty was obstetrics and the care of women and children. During her fifty years of service to communities throughout Utah, Ellis helped deliver more than 6,000 babies. Her interest in medicine expanded beyond simply practicing the profession into the area of teaching. Early in her career, she resolved to share all she had learned about healthcare with others. It was a goal she realized in June of 1879, with the opening of a school of obstetrics. In 1909, reflecting on why such a school was necessary, Ellis wrote:

> As the domains of Utah were becoming inhabited by enterprising men and women, their needs must be supplied. Our new colonies in this western growing country were in sore need. There was not one in their midst who could understandingly care for expectant mothers. And thus came the urge of imparting this knowledge to women. So often we heard the pitiful stories of suffering and even death of women and children. Precious life sacrificed for the need of intelligent care.

At the request of the president of the Latter-Day Saints Women's Relief Society, Doctor Shipp decided to travel to other states and countries to teach women the fundamentals of science and the subjects of nursing and obstetrics. Ellis held classes in Mexico, Canada, Arizona, Colorado, and Idaho.

The emphasis Ellis placed on a higher education was not lost on her children. All five of her offspring completed college. Two of her sons and one of her daughters became doctors themselves.

Doctor Ellis Shipp's illustrious medical career officially ended in 1935. At that time she was honored by her alma mater. Board members and the staff at the Philadelphia Medical College acknowledged her work in a commencement celebration. Her pioneering efforts as a woman doctor were praised, and they noted that her efforts had had a major impact on the welfare of the women and children of the West.

On January 3, 1939, Doctor Shipp passed away quietly in her sleep. She was ninety-two years old.

# FRANC JOHNSON NEWCOMB

## NAVAJO MEDICINE WOMAN

*And swiftly we pass twixt earth and sky, the wind, the dust, the leaf and I.*

—Franc Johnson Newcomb, 1965

Brilliant sunlight poured in through the numerous windows of the Pesh-do-Clish trading post and danced on the merchandise stacked neatly on the shelves. The popular mercantile sat at the tip of the Blue Mesa on the Navajo Reservation near Gallup, New Mexico. The trading post offered a wide variety of products from kerosene lamps, enamel pots, fresh mutton, and washbasins, to jewelry, clothing, and taffy. Such goods were exchanged for hard currency, or rugs, wool, or pinon nuts. The store was not only a place where patrons shopped, but it served as a community center and dispensary as well.

Doctor Franc Johnson Newcomb, a thirty-year-old woman from Pennsylvania, worked behind the counter helping customers with their purchases and discussing the day's news or lack thereof. The special attention she gave her Native-American clientele extended beyond their patronage; she also served as a "healer" for the Navajo.

Among the Navajo, Franc was known as Atsay Ashon, or "the medicine woman." Doctors in remote western territories in the

MEDICINE WOMAN FRANC JOHNSON NEWCOMB WITH
NAVAJO MEDICINE MAN HOSTEEN KLAH IN FRONT OF
THE TRADING POST IN 1936.

1920s were rare, and female physicians were an even greater anomaly. Franc had lived and worked alongside the Navajo for six years. She was well respected and admired, and her two young daughters were treated with equal kindness.

During brief moments between customers, Franc set aside her ledger and medical charts, and stared fondly out the store's open door at the beauty of the desert and mountains. While admiring the vast landscape, she eavesdropped on a conversation her children were having with an elderly Navajo woman. The girls had been studying a spider building its web, and were debating over who would squash the bug first. The Indian woman intervened before either of the girls had a chance to take the spider's life.

"Now don't you bother that spider," she warned. "Spiders are our friends." The quizzical look on the children's faces prompted the woman to explain her comment. "It was Mrs. Spider who taught the Navajo to spin fine thread of leaf fibers, cotton, and wool, and how to weave these threads into blankets and other useful articles," she said.

The girls turned their attention back to the spider and watched it diligently working. "And it is Mrs. Spider who catches flies, mosquitoes, and other flying insects in her web so they don't bother us," the woman added. Franc looked over at the wise elder and smiled. She had herself always wondered why the Navajo never killed spiders and was just as fascinated with the reason as her daughters.

To fully emphasize the consequences of ending a spider's life, the woman concluded her short tale with a warning. "Mrs. Spider has teeth sharp as needle points which slant backwards so her prey has no chance to escape. If a child kills a spider, its second teeth will be crooked." The children stared, wide-eyed, at the woman and then back at the spider. The girls then sprang to their feet and hurried off to find another activity. The Navajo woman watched the spider for a few minutes and then returned to her shopping, satisfied with her efforts to save a living creature.

Franc loved the customs and beliefs of the people that surrounded her. It had not been what brought her to the reservation, but it was in part why she stayed. She became a doctor to bring aid to the sick and suffering, wherever she was needed, and found her place among a people who taught her that there was more to healthcare than she had learned in school.

Born on March 30, 1887, in Tunnel City, Wisconsin, Franc was one of three children born to Frank and Priscilla Johnson. Frank was an architect, and Priscilla was a teacher. Historians believe that Franc's initial interest in medicine began with her parents. Both Frank and Priscilla suffered, and later died, from tuberculosis. Franc was two when her father passed away and twelve when her mother died. Their tragic deaths ignited a passion within Franc to learn about the disease and find a cure.

After their parents' deaths, the three Johnson offspring went to live with their grandparents on a dairy farm in Cable, Wisconsin. It was there Franc completed her primary education and attended high school, graduating in 1904. In the fall of that same year, she enrolled at the Wisconsin Sparta Normal School, and in a year's time she had earned a teaching degree. After graduation she took a job as a teacher at a school in her hometown. The faces of the eager children who had come to learn inspired her. She longed to see that same look on disadvantaged children who wanted an education as well. That desire led her to a one-room schoolhouse on a reservation in Northern Wisconsin. For two years she taught Menominee Indian children how to read, write, add, and subtract.

Franc enjoyed her job and the people around her and immersed herself in the Menominee culture, learning their customs and their language. A persistent cough cast a dark cloud over Franc's time on the reservation, however. As it worsened, fear that she might be suffering from consumption forced her to make a move. She felt her health would improve if she relocated to a drier climate. News of teaching positions being offered out West through the U.S. Civil Service piqued her interest. In 1912, after passing the civil service exam, she moved to Arizona to begin a new teaching job and hopefully conquer her cough in the arid desert.

The Navajo Reservation at Fort Defiance, Arizona, would be Franc's home for more than two years. Her situation paid $25 a month and included room and board at the local mission and trading post. Not long after she arrived in the Southwest, she met the man who would become her husband, Arthur Newcomb. Arthur was the trading post clerk, and he and Franc crossed paths daily. After a brief courtship, the pair married on June 30, 1914. Arthur then purchased a half interest in a New Mexico trading post and moved his bride to their new home on the Navajo Reservation, where the Pesh-do-Clish trading post was located.

When Franc first saw the business, a brilliant sun was washing over the adobe structure. A wooden sign hanging next to the building read PESH-DO-CLISH TRADING POST, and it swayed back and forth in the hot breeze. Gila monsters and jackrabbits were traveling the same desert path Franc and Arthur were using to get to their new home, nestled at the foot of the Blue Mesa Mountains. Arthur stopped the carriage in front of the two-room trading post and helped his wife out of the vehicle. Franc smiled a hopeful smile as she drank in the sight before her.

FRANC JOHNSON NEWCOMB ON HER WEDDING DAY IN 1914.

The post was located 13 miles from the nearest white settler, and was without any direct means of communication. Mule teams brought supplies and the mail to them once a month. Franc was apprehensive at first about the remote setting of their business, but believed in time her life at the trading post would prove to be an amazing adventure.

She wasted no time in transforming the poorly maintained structure into a livable home. After she had dusted and swept, and filled the cracks in the walls, she battled an army of insects that fought to invade the post. A mixture of linseed oil and kerosene, generously applied to the log walls, kept the tarantulas, wood ticks, and centipedes at bay.

The Newcombs' Navajo neighbors were kind and genuinely glad to have them on the reservation. Franc became friends with most of the Indians who shopped at the post and, when needed, she helped care for their children and the elderly. Moved by Franc's compassion toward his people, a medicine man named Hosteen Klah befriended the young teacher and introduced her to the Navajo's traditional way of dealing with health issues. Franc was fascinated with the religious art of healing and attentively listened to Klah's remedies for a variety of ailments.

Klah's process of diagnosis was of particular interest to Franc because the questions asked of a patient went beyond the realm of physical symptoms. "Why is he sick?" Klah would inquire. "What does he eat? What does he hide from himself?" he would further probe. "The patient may move too fast, too quick," Klah explained to Franc. "The body will describe and reveal what the mind is doing."

Klah spent many evenings at the Newcombs' home, dining with them and teaching Franc not only about medicine, but how to better speak the language. He was a wise man who respected traditions of other cultures, even bringing Franc a gift on her wedding day as was the custom among the settlers.

Franc's association with Hosteen Klah elevated her position with the Navajo people. She was seen as a member of the tribe, and she and Arthur were asked to attend weddings, horse races, and feasts. As Klah's apprentice of sorts, Franc was granted access to healing ceremonies too. Such a privilege was rarely granted to women, especially white women. Franc's first experience at such a ceremony left a lasting impression, one that she would write about quite extensively later in her life.

The elaborate healing ceremony is held inside a dome-shaped hogan. The medicine man is seated in a place of honor, near a fire burning in the center of the room. He is surrounded by twelve or so chanters, medicine bags, prayer plumes, and rattles. Tiny particles of ground sand in a variety of colors are placed before the healer. The sand is used to create a special painting.

The medicine man sifts the powdered sand through his fingers, making designs and images on the ground. All the images have significant meanings. Some represent animals or insects; others represent thunder or lighting. Made to strict specifications, the sand painting acts as a homing beacon, drawing out Navajo ancestors and infusing the sacred space with healing powers.

Prayers are offered, rattles are shaken, and chants are sung. The ailing patient is then placed in the center of the complex artwork, where he rubs himself with the various grains from the images. The Navajo people believe the sand paintings helped to restore a cosmic balance to the body.

After the ritual Franc sketched the people involved with the ceremony and made note of their various duties. She also drew the sand paintings, although she felt she could not do justice to the vibrant hues and intricate patterns she witnessed. Klah helped her not only to re-create the sand paintings, but also to understand the meaning behind each figure and image, and how it could heal the sick or hurting. In time she was able to perform the ceremony herself, which added to the respect the Navajo tribe had for her.

In February 1920, a fierce winter storm assaulted the area. Food was scarce due to the harsh freeze that had destroyed livestock and vegetation. Sickness spread throughout the sixteen million acres of Indian land, and hundreds were dying as a result. Franc acquired medical supplies from a government doctor, along with instructions on how to handle such an epidemic. She combined that knowledge with Klah's teachings and set out to make the sick better. In her book, *Navajo Folk Tales,* Franc described the dismal situation:

> *It has been estimated that one-tenth of the Navajo population died that winter, and I believe the estimate is far too low. After the epidemic had passed its peak, the agent at Shiprock sent out teams of men to bury the corpses and burn the death hogans.*

Franc's reputation as a legitimate medicine woman was further enhanced by her administration of such safe products as cough syrup, cod-liver oil, and zinc ointment. Her efforts helped save thousands of Navajo lives.

Having proven herself to be a successful healer, Franc was welcome to all sand-painting ceremonies. In 1920, six years after she had come to live on the reservation, she was officially inducted into the tribe.

Franc was proud of her adopted family and desired to share the beauty of Navajo sand paintings with people outside of the reservation. During her time at the Pesh-do-Clish trading post, Franc had collected many ceremonial artifacts, written down hundreds of religious chants, and drawn more than 700 sand-painting drawings and watercolors. A visiting friend persuaded Franc to display the pieces in a museum. That idea blossomed into the creation of the Museum of Navajo Ceremonial Art in Santa Fe, New Mexico (now known as the Wheelwright Museum). Franc was not content to share the collection only with museum visitors so she wrote a series of books featuring sand paintings, Navajo folk tales, and facts about the culture.

In 1935, Franc and Arthur purchased a home in Albuquerque, New Mexico. Arthur commuted back and forth from home to the trading post, and Franc launched a career as a writer and lecturer on Navajo history, legends, and religion. Disaster struck the Newcombs the following year when a fire broke out at the trading post. The building and all its contents burned to the ground. The store was rebuilt, but Arthur could never get past the emotional impact left behind from the blaze.

Ten years after the inferno destroyed some of his most precious belongings, Arthur died of cirrhosis of the liver. Franc then sold the trading post and devoted her time and money to philanthropic ventures such as the Albuquerque Little Theatre and the New Mexico Museum. She continued to author books about the Navajo influence on the Southwest, and she contributed poetry to various regional publications on the same subject.

Diabetes and cancer ravaged Franc's body when she was in her late seventies, and painful arthritis limited her ability to write. The last book she penned about the Indian tribe to which she proudly belonged was published on July 23, 1970. Franc Johnson Newcomb, the Navajo Medicine Woman, died on July 25, 1970. She was eighty-four years old.

# FLORA HAYWARD STANFORD

## FIRST WOMAN DOCTOR OF DEADWOOD

*Dr. Stanford visited Mr. Inman at the mouth of Nevada Gulch yesterday, and today she again went to visit Mr. Inman, who was very low. Dr. Stanford has hopes of his pulling through if he can hang on for a few days.*

—*Black Hills Daily Times*, August 1893

The rough-and-tumble town of Deadwood, South Dakota, was home to a variety of notorious western characters in the mid-1800s. Buffalo Bill Cody, Wild Bill Hickok, and Calamity Jane were just a few of the infamous names associated with the gold-mining camp. These three legends of the West were at one time patients of the first woman doctor in the area, Doctor Flora Hayward Stanford.

Doctor Stanford opened a practice in Deadwood in 1888 and began seeing to the healthcare needs of hundreds of prospectors, prostitutes, business owners, and their families. She entered the medical profession late in her life, receiving her degree from Boston University School of Medicine in 1878, at the age of forty. Doctor Stanford established her first practice in Washington, D.C., where she lived with her husband, Valentine Stanford, and their two children, Emma and Victor.

Having a doctor for a wife upset Valentine's traditional sense of family. He did not agree with his wife's work and considered it "unseemly for a woman to be a doctor."

The Stanfords decided to separate after their daughter was diagnosed with tuberculosis. Convinced the dry South Dakota climate would help restore Emma's health, Doctor Stanford decided to move to Deadwood. She left her marriage and her son behind in Pennsylvania.

According to historical records, Doctor Stanford was a well-respected physician and the only female doctor in Deadwood at the time. She would travel to patients' homes in a horse and buggy and administer treatment, often for little or no pay. Her standard fee was two to three dollars for an office visit and three to six dollars for a house call. Given the town's proclivity for violence, it wasn't uncommon for Doctor Stanford to be called upon to patch up citizens involved in gunfights. In a letter to her son Victor, she described a particularly brutal incident that left a lasting impression. "A nameless man burst into the office badly shot up," she wrote. "I removed three bullets from his body, dressed his wounds, and permitted him to leave via the rear door of my office," she added. Moments after the man made his getaway, the county sheriff appeared at her door, inquiring after him.

Once the sheriff disclosed the notorious gunfighter's identity to her, he took off after the injured man. "On several occasions," Doctor Stanford confessed to her son, "I had removed one bullet from a man, but this was the first time I had ever removed three at one time."

In spite of the expert care Doctor Stanford lavished on her daughter, Emma's health did not improve. In hopes that a move further west would help her condition, Doctor Stanford closed her office and relocated to Southern California. Emma's condition continued to deteriorate however, and she died in 1893.

Grieving and alone, Doctor Stanford returned to Deadwood,

the place she called home, and resumed her practice. She simultaneously operated a second practice in Sundance, Wyoming, as well. The distance between Sundance and Deadwood was 50 miles, and Doctor Stanford traveled back and forth on horseback to tend to patients in both locations.

In 1897, she purchased a homestead on the Double D Ranch in Wyoming. In addition to maintaining her two medical practices, she was also now working her land.

The labor involved in keeping up with all three projects was overwhelming at times, and her health began to suffer from the effort. On February 1, 1901, Doctor Stanford died of heart complications at age sixty-two. Funeral services were conducted at her graveside with her son Victor and many of her friends and patients in attendance. A *Deadwood Pioneer Times* article, published shortly after her death, lamented the loss:

> *Notwithstanding that she has busied herself with her profession and domestic life, yet she has taken a lively interest in public affairs, she has been prominent in the work of the churches and societies, and her name has been associated in one way or another with almost every laudable enterprise in the city where her assistance was welcome. She was for a number of years a member of the Board of Education of Deadwood, and in that capacity she rendered a valuable service. . . . Tenderly the last offices were performed and the form of her who had been mother, friend, and medical advisor to numbers of struggling and benighted souls was lowered into the narrow home amid a flood of silent tears.*

A plaque honoring her contributions hangs in the main reading room of Deadwood's public library.

# FRONTIER MEDICINE

In the early 1850s, pioneers invaded the majestic plains west of the Mississippi, hauling with them every conceivable provision necessary for life on the new frontier. Among the supplies the emigrants brought along were tents and bedding, cooking utensils, furniture, tools, and extra clothing. Most, if not all, of the items listed could be abandoned if necessary to lighten the load and make room for essentials such as food and medicine.

Women on the wagon trains were responsible not only for preparing the food and making it last through the journey but were also in charge of overall healthcare for the others. Armed with herbal medicine kits and journals filled with remedies, women administered doses of juniper berries, garlic, and bitter roots to cure the ailing. These "granny remedies," as they were called, were antidotes for a variety of illnesses from nausea to typhoid. They were a combination of superstition, religious beliefs, and advice passed down from generation to generation.

Not only did female doctors have to withstand prejudice against their sex, they also had to fight against barbaric remedies that had been passed down from generation to generation. Myths—such as believing a person could preserve his teeth and eliminate mouth odor by rinsing his mouth every morning with his own urine, or that mold scraped from cheese could heal open sores—had to be dispelled.

Some medicines, like herb teas and drawing poultices, brought relief, but most had no effect at all. Indeed many of these remedies did more harm than good. Arsenic, for example, was used to treat heart palpitations and syphilis. Cod-liver oil and onion stew were used to help tuberculosis sufferers, and egg whites and beeswax were used to treat burns. Many of the remedies were based on false notions acquired from ancient books, which instructed sufferers to cure sore throats, for instance, by wearing a piece of bacon sprinkled with black pepper around the neck.

A list of frontier remedies assembled by the Missouri State Historical Society shows why historians refer to this time period as the "Golden Age of Medical Quackery."

- The hot blood of chickens cures shingles.
- Tea made from the scrapings of stallion hooves cures hives.
- Wrap legs in brown paper soaked in vinegar to relieve aching muscles.
- Gold filings in honey restore energy.
- Carry a horse chestnut to ward off rheumatism.
- Watermelon seeds boiled in water help eliminate kidney troubles.
- Sassafras tea thickens the blood.
- The juice of a green walnut cures ringworms.
- Treat chapped hands with salve of kerosene and beef tallow.
- Use a mashed potato poultice to draw out the core of a boil.
- To remove warts, rub them with green walnuts, bacon rind, or chicken feet.
- Use the ointment of crushed sheep sorrel leaves and

gunpowder for skin cancer.

- Mashed snails and earthworms in water are good for diphtheria.
- Common salt with scrapings from pewter spoons for treating worms.
- Boiled pumpkin seed tea for stomach worms.
- Scorpion oil as a diuretic in venereal disease.
- Tea made from steeping dried chicken gizzard linings in hot water for stomachaches.
- Use wood ashes or cobwebs to stop excessive bleeding.
- Brandy and red pepper for cholera.
- Use mold scraped from cheese or old bread for open sores.
- Carry an onion in your pocket to prevent smallpox.
- Wear a bag of asafetida around the neck to cure a cold.
- The oil of geese, wolves, bears, or polecats are good for rheumatism.
- Use the salve of lard and brimstone for an itch.
- Mashed cabbage for ulcers or cancer of the breast.
- Use two tablespoons of India ink to eliminate tapeworm.
- Onions boiled in molasses are good as a laxative.
- Warm brains of a freshly killed rabbit applied to a teething child's gums will relieve the pain.
- Scratch gums with an iron nail until it bleeds, then drive the nail into a wooden beam to relieve toothaches.
- Owl broth cures whooping cough.
- The blood of a "bessie bug" dropped in the ear will cure an earache.

Oddly enough, rattlesnake bites were handled in the same manner as audiences have seen cowboys treat them in films. The bite wound would be sliced open and the poison would be sucked out. If this were done right away, the patient had a good chance for survival.

Before dentists arrived on the frontier, pioneers suffering with toothaches generally sought help from barbers. If a doctor was available, he would provide whatever care was needed. Generally, the problem was dealt with by extracting the offensive tooth using a pair of crude pliers. Whisky and other alcoholic beverages were the only form of anesthetic available at that time.

Most emigrants who made their way west did not practice any kind of dental care. As a result rotten teeth and bad breath were commonplace. Toothbrushes were available in country stores by the late 1850s, as well as soap and chalk toothpastes. However, not everyone used them. Dentists wouldn't become common on the frontier until the 1870s. The average citizen was completely toothless by the time he or she reached fifty.

# ADVERTISEMENTS
# AND WOMEN PHYSICIANS

*If I had had cholera, hydrophobia, smallpox, or any malignant disease, I could not have been more avoided than I was.*

—Doctor Harriet Hunt, first woman to practice medicine successfully in the United States, 1835

The difficult trek across the plains and deserts of the frontier, to Rocky Mountain destinations and beyond, was viewed by the first women physicians as just another obstacle to overcome on the way to achieving their goal. They wanted to practice medicine and believed they would have a chance to do that in the mining camps and cow towns in the West. Initial attempts to practice their profession sent shock waves through the deeply patriarchal society.

Doctor Elise Pfeiffer Stone was subjected to a barrage of ridicule and criticism after an article about her practice ran in the March 5, 1888, edition of a Nevada City, California newspaper:

LADY PHYSICIAN—MRS. E. STONE, WHO IS, WE LEARN, A THOROUGHLY EDUCATED AND ACCOMPLISHED PHYSICIAN, HAS ESTABLISHED HERSELF IN SELBY FLAT, AND OFFERS HER SERVICES TO THE LADIES OF NEVADA AND VICINITY. SHE IS A GRADUATE OF A GERMAN UNIVERSITY AND HAS ENJOYED CONSIDERABLE PRACTICE, SPEAKS SEVERAL LANGUAGES &C.

Doctor Stone's medical knowledge was challenged publicly and frequently by male colleagues who insisted women were not smart enough to be doctors. Eight months after opening her practice in the Gold Country, her professional reputation was slandered by a local physician. In a lengthy article found in the *Nevada Journal*, Doctor Stone articulately responded to her critics:

*In all my professional career I have not had occasion to defend myself against slander intended to injure my professional reputation before; I have practiced for some time as Physician and Midwife in Germany my native home; in N.Y. City and in Buffalo, N.Y., and have been in the high estimation of the profession and the public so far as I am known, which a reference to Dr. L.A. Wolfe of N.Y. or Professor White of Buffalo will testify. The circumstances which calls forth this card [article] is certain false and slanderous remarks which have come to my ears from one calling himself a physician. The last I heard was a sarcastic remark that "he would like to see me in a difficult case of midwifery."*

*Now it is sympathy with my sex at the cruelties practiced on them by men in medical practice for want of knowledge in the profession, that chiefly induced me to remain here, and if that gentlemen or any other will be kind enough, to present me with a difficult case, I will attend it with a great deal of pleasure, that he and the public may form and estimate of my capacity. I have attended 2000 cases of midwifery, among which, I presume, I have had as difficult cases as have fallen to the share of any physician in the country, but how I performed my duties and with what results, I leave others and time in this country to testify; suffice it to say, I challenge any one or number of physicians to prove*

116

THIS CONTROVERSIAL ADVERTISEMENT APPEARED IN MANY WOMEN'S MAGAZINES IN 1891. IT SHOWS THE PROGRESS WOMEN WERE MAKING IN MALE-DOMINATED FIELDS, INCLUDING THE MEDICAL PROFESSION.

*me inferior, in female practice, to any physician in California. My
diploma can be seen at my residence, which will testify that in
midwifery, medical operations, and the use of instruments in all
forms required in medical practice, I have perfected my studies to
the satisfaction and unanimous approbation of the whole board of
professors. Medicines and supporting instruments of all kinds
required by females to be had at my residence.*

The doctor who impugned Elise's reputation was unable to
"prove her inferior" in female practice. He refrained from speaking
out against Doctor Stone again.

In time, women physicians would prove to rugged pioneers
that they were fully capable. Their abilities eventually became so
well respected that the arrivals of female doctors were listed in daily
newspapers. However, the mention of their presence out West came
with just as much insult to their "feminine" qualities as it did praise
for their skills as physicians. An 1864 California newspaper article
hinted that women physicians were essentially stripped of their
"gentler qualifications" by virtue of their career choice:

*Among the arrivals in San Francisco by the last mail steamer
was Miss Sarah Pellet, M.D., a graduate of Oberlin College, a regular educated physician, and an accepted lecturer upon "Women's
Rights" and kindred subjects. Miss Pellet is, we suppose, of the
style of women denominated "strong minded," and is said to pos-
sess a decidedly intellectual cast of thought. The recent Women's
Rights gatherings and conventions in the Atlantic cities have
brought out a large number of the class spoken of, who are stump-
ing it through the Atlantic towns and cities, detailing the real and
imaginary wrongs of women, and proclaiming her inalienable
right to drive omnibuses, command steamboats, preach, make laws*

*and boots and horse shoes, and enter upon all the fields of life which have been heretofore monopolized by the sterner sex.*

*These women (for they scorn the term "ladies") are usually gifted with a greater degree of masculine intellect than the majority of their sex; while from their very appearance it will be at once seen that they are woefully lacking in those gentler qualifications which constituted the charm of "Heaven's last, best gift to man." The inculcation of their doctrines has only a mischievous tendency, and none for good; making a married man's foes those of his own household, and setting up a claim for supremacy where, by the law of nature and of God, obedience is due. Sorry should we be to see the time when "strong minded" women shall take the place of those gentle beings who now, through the civilized world, sit like angels at the domestic hearth, calming the stronger passions of man, and pouring the healing balm of consolation into the wounds which hard rubbing with the world inflict upon those who are called to battle with it.*

In the beginning, the prejudice female doctors encountered was displayed by women as well as men. Many women felt they would be better served by male doctors, who were taken seriously as professionals. A female doctor, by contrast, was considered merely a healer—unable to determine what was really wrong with a patient.

In hopes of dispelling that stereotype, women touted their expertise in a variety of publications. The following ad, for instance, appeared in a February 24, 1882, San Francisco newspaper:

To The Ladies—Madame Costello, Female Physician, still continues to treat, with astonishing success, all diseases peculiar to

FEMALES. SUPPRESSION, IRREGULARITY, OBSTRUCTION, ETC., BY WHATEVER CAUSE PRODUCED, CAN BE REMOVED BY MADAME C IN A VERY SHORT TIME. MADAME C'S MEDICAL ESTABLISHMENT HAVING UNDERGONE THOROUGH REPAIRS AND ALTERATIONS FOR THE BETTER ACCOMMODATION OF HER NUMEROUS PATIENTS, SHE IS NOW PREPARED TO RECEIVE LADIES ON THE POINT CONFINEMENT, OR THOSE WHO WISH TO BE TREATED FOR OBSTRUCTION OF THEIR MONTHLY PERIODS. MADAME C CAN BE CONSULTED AT HER RESIDENCE, 34 LISPENARD STREET.

Female doctors not only advertised their businesses but emphasized medications geared specifically for women. California's *Daily News* ran the following advertisement on April 12, 1843:

MRS. BIRD, FEMALE PHYSICIAN, WHERE CAN BE OBTAINED DR. VANDENBURGH'S FEMALE RENOVATING PILLS, FROM GERMANY, AN EFFECTUAL REMEDY FOR SUPPRESSION, IRREGULARITY, AND ALL CASES WHERE NATURE HAS STOPPED FROM ANY CAUSE WHATEVER. SOLD ONLY AT DOCTOR BIRDS, 83 DUANE STREET NEAR BROADWAY.

By the turn of the century, women physicians had begun to secure a place for themselves among their male peers. They infused a feminine dimension into a profession that arguably would have been less compassionate and more clinical without them.

# BIBLIOGRAPHY

*Albuquerque Journal*, New Mexico, April 14 & 21, 1969.

Allen, T.D. *Doctor in Buckskin*. New York: Harper & Brothers Publishers, 1951.

Alter, Judy. *Pioneer Doctor*. New York: Avon Books, 1980.

Arrington, Leonard and Susan Arrington. *Sunbonnet Sisters: True Stories of Mormon Women and Frontier Life*. Salt Lake City, Utah: Bookcraft Publishers, 1984.

Barnhart, Jan and C.C. O'Hearn. *Medicine Woman: The Women Who Made the West*. New York: Avon Books, 1980.

Bettmann, Otto L. *The Good Old Days—They Were Terrible*. New York: Random House, 1974.

*Black Hills Daily Times*, Deadwood, South Dakota, August 1893.

Blaugh, L.E. "Dentistry as a Career," Chicago Dental Society Newsletter, June 11, 1936.

Brown, Dee. *The Gentle Tamers: Women of the Old Wild West*. Lincoln, Neb.: University of Nebraska Press, 1958.

# BIBLIOGRAPHY

Brown, Leroy W. *History of Patty Bartlett Sessions: Mother of Mormon Midwifery.* North Glenn, Col., self–published, 1975.

Casterline, Gail F. *Ellis R. Shipp: Sister Saints.* Provo, Utah: Brigham Young University Press, 1978.

Chartier, J. and Chris Enss. *With Great Hope: Women of the California Gold Rush.* Guilford, Conn.: Globe Pequot Press, 2000.

Cornell, Virginia. *Doc Susie: The True Story of a Country Physician in the Colorado Rockies.* New York: Ivy Books, 1991.

Doyle, Helen. *A Child Went Forth, or Doctor Nellie: The Autobiography of Dr. Helen MacKnight.* New York: Gotham House Press, 1934.

Dunlop, Richard. *Doctors of the American Frontier.* New York: Doubleday & Company, 1965.

Evans, John Henry. *Joseph Smith: An American Prophet.* New York: MacMillan Co., 1946.

Gates, Susa Y. and Leah Widtsoe. *The Life Story of Brigham Young.* New York: MacMillan Co., 1930.

Hastings, Dennis. *Omaha Tribe Historian.* Omaha, Neb.: Lerner Books, 1991.

"History of the Pacific Northwest," *Ancestry Magazine,* March 17, 2004.

Holmes, Kenneth L., ed. *Covered Wagon Women: Diaries and Letters from the Western Trails, 1840–1890,* Vol. 1. Glendale, Calif.: Arthur H. Clarke Co., 1983.

Karolevitz, Robert. *Doctors of the Old West.* New York: Bonanza Books, 1938.

King, Elizabeth N. "Women in Dentistry," *Washington University Dental Journal,* 1945.

Lo Chin, Eliza. *This Side of Doctoring: Reflections From Women in Medicine.* Thousand Oaks, Calif.: Sage Publications, 2002.

Lockley, Fred. *With Her Own Wings.* Portland, Ore.: Beattie & Company, 1948.

Lopate, Carol. *Women in Medicine.* Baltimore: Johns Hopkins University Press, 1968.

Luchetti, Cathy and Carol Olwell. *Women of the West.* New York: Crown Trade Paperback, 1982.

Luchetti, Cathy. *Medicine Women.* New York: Crown Publishing, Inc., 1998.

McCook, Mor. *Gering, Nebraska: The First One Hundred Years.* Gering, Neb.: Red Willow Press, 1984.

Newcomb, Franc J. *Hosteen Klah: Navajo Medicine Man and Sand Painter.* Norman, Okla.: University of Oklahoma Press, 1964.

————. Navajo Folk Tales. Santa Fe, New Mexico: Museum of Navajo Ceremonial Art, 1967.

*Oregon Historical Quarterly.* Oregon Historical Society. Vol. LXXVIII, No. 1. 1977.

Owens, B.A. *Gleanings From a Pioneer Woman Physician's Life.* Portland, Ore.: Mann & Beach, 1906.

Powers, Marla N. *Oglala Women: Myth, Ritual, and Reality.* Chicago: University of Chicago Press, 1986.

Rezatto, Helen. *Mount Moriah: The Story of Deadwood's Boot Hill.* Rapid City, S.D.: Fenwyn Press, 1989.

Roth Walsh, Mary. *Doctors Wanted: No Women Need Apply: Sexual Barriers in the Medical Profession.* New Haven, Conn.: Yale University Press, 1973.

Rowland, Mary Canaga. *As Long As Life: The Memoirs of a Frontier Woman Physician.* Seattle, Washington: Storm Peak Press, 1994.

*Santa Fe New Mexican,* August 9, 1970.

Sessions, P.B. *Diaries of Patty Bartlett Sessions: Life Writings of Frontier Women.* Logan, Utah: Utah State University Press, 1997.

Shipp, Ellis R. *While Others Slept.* Salt Lake City, Utah: Bookcraft Publishers, 1962.

Skalla, Judy. *Beloved Healer: Women Who Made the West.* New York: Avon Books, 1980.

Stockel, Henrietta and Victoria Krueger. *Medicine Women, Curanderas, and Women Doctors.* Norman, Okla.: University of Oklahoma Press, 1989.

Taylor, Dick. "Stories at Eleven," *Nebraska Heritage Magazine,* December 3, 2000, Vol. 4, No. 47.

*The Ellis Reynolds Shipp Papers.* A Register of the Collection at the Utah State Historical Society, 2000.

*The Gering Courier,* May 1889 and January 22 & 29, 1937.

Tong, Dennis. *Susan La Flesche Picotte, M.D., Omaha Indian Leader and Reformer.* Norman, Okla.: University of Oklahoma Press, 1999.

Tyler, A.F. and E.F. Auerbach. *History of Medicine in Nebraska.* Omaha, Neb.: Magic Printing Company, 1928.

Whitney, Rae E. *A Portrait of Dr. Georgia Arbuckle Fix.* Scottsbluff, Neb.: Figtree Press, 1984.

# ABOUT THE AUTHOR

Chris Enss, an award-winning screen writer who has written for television, short subject films, live performances, and for the movies, is the author of *Hearts West: True Stories of Mail-Order Brides on the Frontier, How the West Was Worn: Bustles and Buckskins on the Wild Frontier,* and *Buffalo Gals: Women of Buffalo Bill's Wild West Show.* She is also the co-author (with JoAnn Chartier) of *With Great Hope: Women of the California Gold Rush, Love Untamed: True Romances Stories of the Old West, Gilded Girls: Women Entertainers of the Old West,* and *She Wore A Yellow Ribbon: Women Patriots and Soldiers of the Old West. The Cowboy and the Senorita* and *Happy Trails* she co-wrote with Howard Kazanjian.

Enss has done everything from stand-up comedy to working as a stunt person at the Old Tucson Movie Studio. She learned the basics of writing for film and television at the University of Arizona, and she is currently working with *Return of the Jedi* producer Howard Kazanjian on the movie version of *The Cowboy and the Senorita,* their biography of western stars Roy Rogers and Dale Evans. Her research and writing and reveals the funny, touching, exciting, and tragic stories of historical and contemporary times.

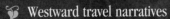